J.J. O'MALLEY

Publications International, Ltd.

Louis Weber, CEO
Publications International, Ltd.
7373 North Cicero Avenue
Lincolnwood, Illinois 60712

ISBN-13: 978-1-4127-1570-6
ISBN-10: 1-4127-1570-9

Manufactured in China.

8 7 6 5 4 3 2 1

Library of Congress Control Number: 2007932014

Credits

The editors gratefully acknowledge the cooperation of the following photographers and sources, without whom this book would not have been possible:

Greg Fielden: 70, 71, 87; **LaDon George:** 88; **Getty Images:** 122-125, back cover; **Bryan Hallman:** 82, 83, 127; **Mike Horne:** 95, 106, 108; **Larry McTighe:** 108, 111; **Bill Niven:** 62; **Publications International, Ltd.:** 24, 82.

All other photography provided by Motorsports Images & Archives.

Special thanks to Ron Koch.

Contents

Introduction

Even in the exciting, fast-paced world of NASCAR racing, the Daytona 500 stands out. Not only is it unquestionably the most flamboyant and famous event of the season, it has been around longer than any other and still carries its original name rather than that of a sponsor. In 1979 it became the first NASCAR race to be televised live, start-to-finish, on a national network, and has consistently scored among the top-rated sporting events every year since.

Though the Daytona 500 is steeped in tradition, much has changed in the nearly 50 years since its inaugural running in 1959. One of the most obvious is the cars that are raced. At first they were nearly stock; today they are anything but. An overview of how and why they've changed is covered in "The Cars of Daytona" section in the back of this book. Also explained is the qualification process for the Daytona 500, which has always been more involved than for any other NASCAR event. That, along with a historical overview of how the Daytona International Speedway came to be, can be found in "The History of Daytona" on the following pages.

We hope those who are eagerly awaiting the 50th running of the Daytona 500 will find that this colorful glimpse at the event's rich history gives this monumental milestone even greater meaning—and clarifies why the Daytona 500 has long been called "The Great American Race."

The History of Daytona

The Daytona 500 became the cornerstone of Daytona International Speedway when the facility opened in 1959. The 50th running of "The Great American Race" will take place in 2008, continuing more than a century of tradition of Central Florida motorsports.

Competition in the Daytona Beach area dates back to 1903, when Alexander Winton raced Horace Thomas as part of a speed trial on the sands of Ormond Beach, just north of Daytona Beach. Over the following decades, Daytona Beach attracted international attention as drivers tested their skill and courage on the hard-packed sand with many land speed record attempts, climaxed by Sir Malcolm Campbell's historic pass of 276 mph in his *Bluebird* in 1935.

Eventually, the Bonneville Salt Flats in Utah became the most popular location for land speed records. To keep Daytona Beach on the map, local officials turned to racing cars and motorcycles on a course using a stretch of beach connected by tight, sandy turns to a section of adjacent highway A1A. One of the competitors in those beach races was "Big Bill" France, who relocated from Washington, D.C., to Daytona Beach in 1934 as a 23-year-old mechanic—and watched Campbell's historic run. After a rough start, France gradually evolved from driver to promoter, and his efforts would forever change the world of auto racing.

France founded NASCAR in 1948, looking to stabilize the rough-and-tumble sport of stock car racing. While his cornerstone event ran at Daytona, promoting beach racing was becoming an increasingly difficult task. Not only did France have to cope with tides and deteriorating conditions, beachside growth and resulting traffic encroached on the races. To ensure continuation of the sport in Daytona Beach, France knew he would have to build a permanent facility, and he began lobbying for a speedway in 1953. It took six years, but it was well worth the wait.

The Track

Compared with other tracks of the day, Daytona International Speedway was an imposing sight. Most NASCAR races were still being held on flat dirt or paved ovals of a mile or less, with only the banked 1.375-mile Darlington Raceway providing real high-speed action. When the 2.5-mile Daytona track opened in 1959, the highest qualifying speed that year at Darlington was 123.734 mph; at Daytona, it was 20 mph faster.

But it wasn't just the blistering lap speeds that intimidated some competitors. Daytona's tall, 31-degree banked corners were like nothing these racers had ever seen. Driver Jimmy Thompson summed it up by saying, "There have been other tracks that separated the men from the boys. This is the track that will separate the brave from the weak after the boys are gone." Indeed, many drivers who were perennial front-runners on the short tracks failed to carry that success over to the high-speed banks of Daytona.

1.

3.

2.

1. The famed 4.15-mile Daytona Beach and Road Course— last used in 1958—boasted two-mile straightaways connected by a pair of tight, sandy turns. 2. An aerial shot shows the Daytona International Speedway grounds during the early stages of construction. Note the track's "tri-oval" shape. 3. Several test runs were made before pavement was laid on the speedway's 31-degree banking. 4. The 2.5-mile speedway is an imposing sight from any angle. 5. Colorful pageantry highlights Daytona's Speedweeks celebration.

4.

5.

The Race

The headlining event at the new track was the inaugural Daytona 500. Like the track itself, the race took drivers into uncharted territory: competing for 500 flat-out, white-knuckled miles on a high-banked oval. The event proved a huge success, highlighted by a finish so close it took 61 hours to determine the winner.

But Bill France intended the Daytona 500 to be more than just a single race. As such, it became the star attraction in a series of events known as "Speedweeks." Traditionally, Speedweeks has been held during February, and since 1982, the Daytona 500 has been the first points race of the NASCAR season.

Qualifying

The procedure for setting the starting lineup for the Daytona 500 is unique in the world of NASCAR racing. At every other event, the cars run one or two laps against the clock to determine their starting positions on the grid. Qualifying at Daytona has always been a more involved process, as drivers not only pit their skills in two laps against the clock, but also have to compete in preliminary events to make the lineup for "The Great American Race."

Originally, the front of the grid for the 500 was set by a traditional qualifying run along with a pair of 100-mile qualifying races. The fastest qualifier earned the pole position in both the first qualifying race and the Daytona 500. The second fastest qualifier got the pole in the second qualifying race and the outside of the front row in the 500. Although their starting positions in the 500 were already set, the two pole sitters were required to at least take the green flag for their qualifying race. While a few drivers parked their cars after one lap in the early years (because if their car was involved in an accident, they would be dropped to the back of the field for the Daytona 500), traditionally the pole sitter would attempt to complete the entire distance.

After each qualifying race was run, the next 14 rows were established by finishing order; those in the first qualifying race filled the inside lane, those in the second race filled the outside lane. Thus, the top 14 finishers in each of the qualifying races—plus the respective pole sitters—made up the top 30 starting positions for the Daytona 500. Following the top 30 starters, the remainder of the 42-car field was filled by the fastest non-qualified cars from time trials,

along with "provisional starters" per the NASCAR rulebook. For many years, these final 12 positions consisted of 10 cars from the time trials, followed by the two provisional starters, which were the top two in car owners' points from the previous year. More recently, as many as seven provisional starters were added to the field. The qualifying races were extended to 125 miles in 1968 and carried full NASCAR point status until 1971. In 1972, races of less than 200 miles were dropped from the NASCAR schedule (thus trimming the number of events from 46 to 31), which meant the qualifying races no longer awarded points toward the championship.

The system for setting the Daytona 500 grid was overhauled in 2004. While pole day still determined the top two starters, the top 35 in the previous year's car-owner points were guaranteed starting positions. This meant that only two drivers from each qualifying race were added to the field—although their finish in the qualifying race determined where they started in the lineup. In 2005, the qualifying races—now known as the Gatorade Duel At Daytona—were increased from 125 miles to 150 miles to ensure that everyone had to pit at least once for fuel during the race.

Joining pole qualifying and the Gatorade Duel At Daytona have been a variety of other events. The ARCA 200, a stock car race for the midwest-based RE/MAX Series, has been a mainstay since 1964. The Budweiser Shootout At Daytona, featuring the previous year's Budweiser Pole Award winners (fastest qualifiers) in a sprint race, debuted as the Busch Clash in 1979. Late Model Sportsman races held the day before the Daytona 500 were replaced by a NASCAR Busch Series race, while a Friday NASCAR Craftsman Truck Series event joined Speedweeks in 2000.

Other major events held at Daytona International Speedway include a second annual NASCAR date in July, the yearly Rolex 24 At Daytona—a major international sports car race—in late January, and the Daytona 200 motorcycle race held during Bike Week in March.

Ask any NASCAR driver what race they'd most like to win, and chances are they'd say—without hesitation—"the Daytona 500." And that's been the case for nearly 50 years. From its inaugural running in 1959, the Daytona 500 has been granted a status of nearly mythical proportions by drivers and fans alike, firmly establishing The Great American Race as the premier event on the annual NASCAR schedule. And that's likely to be the case for the *next* 50 years.

1959

1.

2.

1. In the planning stages since early 1955, construction on the Daytona International Speedway began in 1957. Obtaining the dirt to mold the high-banked, 31-degree turns created a 44-acre borrow pit in the infield. This was dubbed "Lake Lloyd" in honor of local car dealer J. Saxton Lloyd, a major financial contributor to the construction of the speedway. 2. A color postcard depicting the inaugural Daytona 500 featured its high-banked turns, colorful stock cars, and packed grandstands. 3. Richard Petty (#43) leads eventual winner Shorty Rollins (#99), Larry Frank (#76), Marvin Panch (#98), Gene White (#25), Glen Wood (#21), and Wilbur Rakestraw (#92) during the 100-mile qualifying race for NASCAR convertibles. Petty used the newly discovered draft to take the lead down the backstretch on the final lap, only to have it used against him in the sprint to the finish line, during which he fell to third.

3.

4. Thirty-eight cars started the 100-mile qualifying race for NASCAR's premier-series hardtops. The 40-lap event was a wide-open sprint from the start, with cars running at top speed in a variety of grooves. Bob Welborn held off rookie Fritz Wilson to win the race by half a car length at an average speed of 143.198 mph. **5.** Johnny Bruner, Sr., waved the green flag to start the inaugural Daytona 500 while standing on the apron of the track.

4.

5.

RICHARD PETTY
My First Race at Daytona

Racing Daytona for the first time was really different from anything we'd experienced.

The first time we ever ran here was in 1959, when I ran the convertible race. That was the first race ever held here. I was out there with a big 1957 Oldsmobile, running about 130 mph—that's about all it would run. I noticed there were about four or five of us that got away from everybody. Then, when we came up on a group to lap them about maybe halfway through the race, all of a sudden they got to running as fast as we did.

"Man," I said, "there's something going on here—I'm just not sure what it is."

So, on the last lap, I laid back a little, and then passed them all going up the backstretch.

"Man," I said, "this is easy." But, about that time, they caught the draft and two or three of them got back by me before we got to the start/finish line. That was my first drafting experience.

"They had more hardtops than convertibles, so Bill France said he'd give me $1,000 if I cut the top off my car. . . . When they dropped the flag to go, there was so much suction [created by the much faster hardtops blowing by] it felt like it wanted to pull you out. . . . Biggest mistake I ever made!"

—Marvin Panch

1959

1.

2.

1. NASCAR convertibles and premier-series hardtops are shown racing through the third turn in the inaugural Daytona 500. At the high speeds afforded by the long, steeply banked track, the open-top cars proved both unstable and about 10-mph slower than the more streamlined hardtops. It marked the beginning of the end for convertibles in NASCAR; the division closed down later in the year. 2. This shot taken down the home stretch of the first Daytona 500 shows why the finish is famous for being among the most exciting in NASCAR history. Joe Weatherly's #48 Chevrolet (top car) appears to be leading by a nose but is actually two laps down—a fact unknown by the driver, who continued to battle fiercely for the victory. That left it a two-car duel between Lee Petty's #42 Oldsmobile in the center and Johnny Beauchamp's #73 Ford Thunderbird on the inside. It made for what was quite literally a photo finish at the checkered flag. 3. A side-view shot of the finish shows Petty's #42 Oldsmobile half a fender ahead of Beauchamp's #73 T-Bird just before the stripe. 4. Race officials didn't have immediate access to the finish-line photo, and since they thought Beauchamp had crossed the line first, he was handed the trophy. But several people who saw the finish up close thought Petty had won, prompting race officials to hold off on officially declaring a winner. 5. Bill France (left), along with Ed Otto and Dick Dolan, spent hours on end studying photographs and footage of the finish. It wasn't until film from the *Hearst Metrotone News of the Week* arrived and showed conclusively that Petty crossed the finish line first that he was declared the winner—61 hours after the race ended.

3.

4.

5.

Lee Petty #42 Oldsmobile

2. Johnny Beauchamp   Ford
3. Charlie Griffith   Pontiac
4. Cotton Owens   Pontiac
5. Joe Weatherly   Chevrolet
6. Jim Reed   Chevrolet
7. Jack Smith   Chevrolet
8. Tom Pistone   Ford
9. Tim Flock   Ford
10. Speedy Thompson   Chevrolet

100-Mile Qualifying Race winners:
Bob Welborn (Hardtop)
Shorty Rollins (Convertible)

1960

1.

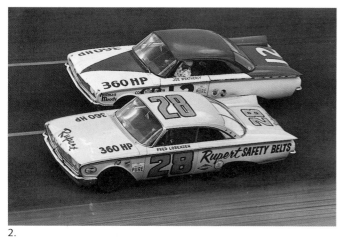

2.

"Winning the Daytona 500 was a big moment in my career. Daytona is the cream of the crop. If you didn't win that race in NASCAR, you did not hav a good career. Winning the Daytona 500 was what it's all about."

—Junior Johnson

1. Pontiacs dominated during time trials and preliminary races at Daytona in 1960. Shown are #6 Cotton Owens, #47 Jack Smith, #22 Fireball Roberts, and #3 Bobby Johns (in a '59 model) leading a Ford and a Chevrolet. Roberts turned in the quickest qualifying speed at 151.556 mph, but Owens started on the point after winning a 25-mile pole-position race. **2.** Fred Lorenzen in the #28 Ford battles Joe Weatherly in the #12 Ford early in the Daytona 500. Lorenzen would later become a superspeedway star, and Weatherly would go on to win two NASCAR championships. **3.** Junior Johnson's Chevrolet is serviced in the pits during the Daytona 500. **4.** Two legends of NASCAR battle side-by-side during the Daytona 500, as Junior Johnson (#27) moves to the inside of Curtis Turner (#26). **5.** Future two-time NASCAR champion Ned Jarrett started his #11 Ford 54th after crashing in his qualifying race but worked his way up to a sixth-place finish. **6.** Junior Johnson enjoys a cold Pepsi as he is joined by car owner and crew chief Ray Fox in Victory Lane ceremonies.

3.

4.

5.

6.

Junior
Johnson #27 Chevrolet

2. Bobby Johns   Pontiac
3. Richard Petty   Plymouth
4. Lee Petty   Plymouth
5. Johnny Allen   Chevrolet
6. Ned Jarrett   Ford
7. Curtis Turner   Ford
8. Fred Lorenzen   Ford
9. Rex White   Chevrolet
10. Emanuel Zervakis   Chevrolet

100-Mile Qualifying Race winners:
Fireball Roberts, Jack Smith

1961

1.

1. Nineteen sixty-one was not a good year for the Pettys at Daytona. Both cars entered were damaged in their respective 100-mile qualifying races, and neither made the field for the Daytona 500. Richard Petty's car (#43) got bumped by Junior Johnson in the first race, while Lee Petty's (right) took a bit more of a hit in the second. **2.** The mishap that sidelined Lee Petty involved the two principles from the historic finish of the inaugural Daytona 500. Petty (#42) got tagged from behind by Johnny Beauchamp (#73), and both cars were heavily damaged. Neither driver was able to compete in the 500. **3.** Fireball Roberts, driving Smokey Yunick's black and gold #22 Pontiac, leads the field through the banking on the parade lap of the 1961 Daytona 500. Joe Weatherly (#8) starts on the outside of the front row, with Jim Paschal (#3) and Marvin Panch (#20) in the second row. **4.** Marvin Panch, driving Smokey Yunick's year-old #20 Pontiac, battles a pair of Fords—including Banjo Matthews' #94—and a Pontiac during the 500. **5.** Legendary car builder/mechanic Smokey Yunick poses with Marvin Panch and the year-old Pontiac that Panch drove in the 500. Unlike the Pettys, Yunick had a bit of luck at Daytona. Fireball Roberts dominated the race in a new Yunick-built Pontiac, leading all but 17 laps before blowing an engine with only 13 laps remaining. However, second-place runner Marvin Panch drove Yunick's older Pontiac and breezed to the win. **6.** Flanked by a pair of race queens, a happy Marvin Panch waves to the crowd during Victory Lane cer-

2.

3.

4.

5.

6.

Marvin Panch #20 Pontiac

2. Joe Weatherly   Pontiac
3. Paul Goldsmith   Pontiac
4. Fred Lorenzen   Ford
5. Cotton Owens   Pontiac
6. Jack Smith   Pontiac
7. Ned Jarrett   Chevrolet
8. Johnny Allen   Chevrolet
9. Buck Baker   Chrysler
10. Tom Pistone   Pontiac

100-Mile Qualifying Race winners:
Fireball Roberts, Joe Weatherly

1962

1.

2.

3.

4.

1. Daytona Beach resident Glenn "Fireball" Roberts had his fastball working during 1962 Speedweeks. Roberts ran the table, winning the pole position, his 100-mile qualifying race, and the Daytona 500. He poses with the winning #22 Pontiac prepared by Smokey Yunick, also of Daytona Beach. 2. After sitting out the 1961 Daytona 500 due to a pair of crashes, Petty Enterprises returned in 1962 with a pair of Plymouths. While Richard Petty drove the #43, his father, Lee Petty, turned the #42 over to Bunkie Blackburn. The elder Petty saw only limited action over the following seasons before retiring in 1964 with a then-record 54 NASCAR victories. 3. Fireball Roberts (#22) runs with Bobby Jones (#72) and Jack Smith (#47) at the start of the Daytona 500. 4. Fireball Roberts' #22 Pontiac provides a draft for Richard Petty's #43 Plymouth as they pass the #01 Ford of Billy Wade. Petty's Plymouth was no match for Roberts' fleet Pontiac, but Petty made the most of the suction created by the draft and rode Roberts' coattails to a second-place finish. 5. The other Petty Enterprises Plymouth, the #42 of Bunkie Blackburn, was less able to benefit from Roberts' draft and finished 13th. 6. Fireball Roberts celebrates the biggest of his 33 NASCAR victories, the 1962 Daytona 500.

5.

6.

Fireball Roberts #22 Pontiac

2.	Richard Petty	Plymouth
3.	Joe Weatherly	Pontiac
4.	Jack Smith	Pontiac
5.	Fred Lorenzen	Ford
6.	David Pearson	Pontiac
7.	Rex White	Chevrolet
8.	Banjo Matthews	Pontiac
9.	Ned Jarrett	Chevrolet
10.	Bob Welborn	Pontiac

100-Mile Qualifying Race winners:
Fireball Roberts, Joe Weatherly

1963

1.

2.

3.

1. Marvin Panch was involved in a crash of a Birdcage Maserati-Ford at Daytona International Speedway 10 days prior to the Daytona 500. Tiny Lund, who was rideless for the 500, helped pull him from the burning car. Panch's injuries prevented him from driving in the 500, and legend has it that Lund was rewarded with the ride in Panch's Ford for the race. However, the Wood Brothers team said they gave it to Lund because he was the best available driver. Regardless, Lund won the race to complete a Cinderella story. **2.** A.J. Foyt, the reigning Indianapolis 500 winner, made his second NASCAR start in his 100-mile qualifying race, finishing third in the #02 Ray Nichels Pontiac. He spun out in the 500 and finished 27th. Foyt made his NASCAR debut at Riverside, California, in January 1963, finishing second behind Dan Gurney. **3.** The field takes the green flag for the second 100-mile qualifying race for the 1963 Daytona 500. Fred Lorenzen (#28) leads from the pole, with Tiny Lund (#21) on the outside and Ned Jarrett (#11) starting third. Eventual winner Johnny Rutherford started ninth, the fifth car on the inside lane. **4.** Johnny Rutherford, holding the trophy, talks with car owner Smokey Yunick after winning the second Twin 100-mile qualifying race. Yunick wanted to put an unknown driver in his car for the race. Rutherford's performance helped him launch a hall-of-fame career driving Indy Cars. He was the last rookie to win a Daytona qualifying race until Jeff Gordon did it in 1993. **5.** Ned Jarrett (#11) attempts to pass Tiny Lund (#21) on the inside during the closing laps of the Daytona 500. Pit strategy by the Wood Brothers resulted in Lund being able to run the race with one less pit stop than his rivals. When Jarrett needed to pit with three laps remaining, Lund coasted to a 24-second victory over Fred Lorenzen. "We knew we were going to win the race unless the gas tank blew up or something," Leonard Wood later stated.

4.

5.

Tiny
Lund #21 Ford

2. Fred Lorenzen   Ford
3. Ned Jarrett   Ford
4. Nelson Stacy   Ford
5. Dan Gurney   Ford
6. Richard Petty   Plymouth
7. Bobby Johns   Pontiac
8. Joe Weatherly   Pontiac
9. Johnny Rutherford   Chevrolet
10. Tommy Irwin   Ford

100-Mile Qualifying Race winners:
Junior Johnson, Johnny Rutherford

1964

1.

2.

1. The Pontiac pace car pulls onto pit road seconds before the start of the 1964 Daytona 500. Pole winner Paul Goldsmith (#25) is joined by Richard Petty (#43) on the front row, with Junior Johnson (#3) and Bobby Isaac (#26) in row two. Coming through the pack are A.J. Foyt (#00) and David Pearson (#6). **2.** Ford drivers Fred Lorenzen (#28) and Larry Frank (#29) battle during the Daytona 500. Lorenzen earned the nickname "Golden Boy" in 1963, when he won six races and shattered the magic $100,000 mark by winning $122,588—an incredible sum at the time. But he and the other Ford drivers struggled at Daytona. Lorenzen cut a tire and finished 17th in his qualifying race, then blew an engine on lap 49 and placed 31st in the Daytona 500. **3.** Richard Petty's #43 Plymouth is serviced during the Daytona 500. Note tire changer Maurice Petty's color-coordinated boots.

3.

4.

4. Richard Petty hit his stride in the 1964 Daytona 500. He led 460 of the 500 miles, lapping the field in the process. Chasing the Petty Blue #43 Plymouth are eventual runner-up Jimmy Pardue (#54), the Ray Nichels #26 Dodge driven by Bobby Isaac, and the #25 Nichels Plymouth piloted by Paul Goldsmith. **5.** Richard Petty's #43 Plymouth takes the checkered flag to win the Daytona 500, his first superspeedway victory. He beat Jimmy Pardue by one lap plus nine seconds after leading all but 16 of the 200 laps. **6.** While well-wishers gather around the #43 Plymouth, Richard Petty accepts the winner's trophy from Miss Japan, Akiko Kajima.

5.

6.

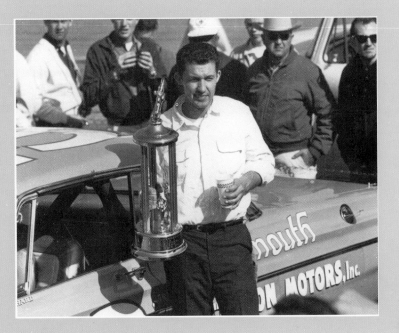

Richard Petty #43 Plymouth

2.	Jimmy Pardue	Plymouth
3.	Paul Goldsmith	Plymouth
4.	Marvin Panch	Dodge
5.	Jim Paschal	Dodge
6.	Billy Wade	Mercury
7.	Darel Dieringer	Mercury
8.	Larry Frank	Ford
9.	Junior Johnson	Dodge
10.	Dave MacDonald	Mercury

100-Mile Qualifying Race winners:
Junior Johnson, Bobby Isaac

1.

2.

3.

4.

1. Junior Johnson (#27) and Fred Lorenzen (#28) race side-by-side during the second qualifying race of the 1965 Daytona Speedweeks. Johnson won when Lorenzen slowed after taking the white flag, thinking the race had ended. **2.** Junior Johnson tightens his helmet as he prepares for another race. Author Tom Wolfe wrote about Johnson in a 1964 *Esquire* magazine article entitled "Junior Johnson is the Last American Hero. Yes!" **3.** When NASCAR outlawed the Hemi engine for 1965 on the grounds it gave racers an unfair

advantage, many Dodge and Plymouth teams boycotted the season. Richard Petty kept his competitive juices flowing by drag racing the #43 Plymouth Barracuda. **4.** Ned Jarrett (#11) leads Jerry Grant (#72) and Dick Hutcherson (#29) during the Daytona 500. Jarrett won 13 races in 1965 en route to his second NASCAR title. He hung up his helmet at the end of the following season at age 34. **5.** After leading the opening 27 laps of the 1965 Daytona 500, Junior Johnson cut a tire and

5.

crashed his #27 Ford on lap 28 of what would be his last 500. Racing by are Sam McQuagg (#24), Don Tilley (#81), and Doug Cooper (#60). **6.** Fred Lorenzen (#28) was leading on lap 133 when rain red-flagged the 500. Three hours later he was declared the winner. Marvin Panch was his toughest rival. The 1961 winner led three times but lost a lap after tangling with Lorenzen and finished sixth.

6.

Fred Lorenzen #28 Ford

2. Darel Dieringer	Mercury
3. Bobby Johns	Ford
4. Earl Balmer	Mercury
5. Ned Jarrett	Ford
6. Marvin Panch	Ford
7. Dick Hutcherson	Ford
8. Sam McQuagg	Ford
9. Cale Yarborough	Ford
10. G.C. Spencer	Ford

100-Mile Qualifying Race winners:
Darel Dieringer, Junior Johnson

1966

1.

2.

1. Paul Goldsmith (left) made headlines by winning the first of the Twin 100-mile qualifying races at the 1966 Daytona Speedweeks. Earl Balmer (right) took his only NASCAR trophy for winning the second race. Both drivers won on last-lap passes. Neither were as lucky in the Daytona 500. Goldsmith finished 18th, while Balmer retired on lap 21 with engine trouble. **2.** Junior Johnson went from driver to car owner in 1966, fielding the #26 Ford for Bobby Isaac; it's shown getting service during the Daytona 500. Isaac finished seventh in his qualifying race but crashed and placed 21st in the 500. **3.** A crowd of 90,000 watched the green flag wave for the 1966 Daytona 500. Richard Petty (#43) is joined by Dick Hutcherson (#29) on the front row, followed by Paul Goldsmith (#99) and Earl Balmer (#3). **4.** Curtis Turner (left) finished 25th in a Ford fielded by the Wood Brothers. Darel Dieringer (right) finished 12th in a Bud Moore Mercury. **5.** Richard Petty (#43) chases Cale Yarborough's #27 Banjo Matthews Ford. Between them, the pair would win a total of 11 Daytona 500s. Yarborough went on to finish second, one lap behind Petty. Also in the battle is Paul Goldsmith, driving Ray Nichels' #99 Plymouth. **6.** With cars throwing rooster tails of spray, Richard Petty takes the checkered flag at the end of lap 198 to win the 1966 Daytona 500. The race was ended two laps early due to a downpour. **7.** Richard Petty holds a pair of giant trophies as reward for winning his second 500, making him the first driver to win two.

3.

4.

5.

6.

7.

Richard Petty #43 Plymouth

2. Cale Yarborough — Ford
3. David Pearson — Dodge
4. Fred Lorenzen — Ford
5. Sam McQuagg — Dodge
6. Jim Hurtubise — Plymouth
7. Ned Jarrett — Ford
8. LeeRoy Yarbrough — Dodge
9. James Hylton — Dodge
10. Larry Frank — Plymouth

100-Mile Qualifying Race winners:
Paul Goldsmith, Earl Balmer

1967

1.

2.

3.

4.

5.

1. Curtis Turner put Smokey Yunick's #13 Chevrolet on the pole for the 1967 Daytona 500 and quit his qualifying race after only one lap because he felt the car was ready. He led the 500 twice for six laps before exiting with a blown engine on lap 144. **2.** The field readies for the start of the first qualifying race for the Daytona 500. Pole winner Curtis Turner, in Smokey Yunick's #13 Chevrolet, is joined by the #6 Dodge Charger of David Pearson. LeeRoy Yarbrough, the eventual winner of this qualifying race, is on the inside of the second row in the #12 Dodge. Next to him is A.J. Foyt's #27 Ford, followed by the #71 Dodge of Bobby Isaac and the #3 Dodge of Buddy Baker. **3.** Fred Lorenzen waves to the crowd after winning the second Twin 100 qualifying race of the 1967 Daytona Speedweeks. It was his final NASCAR victory. **4.** Mario Andretti, driving the #11 Holman-Moody Ford, leads the #6 Cotton Owens Dodge of David Pearson and the #42 Petty Enterprises Plymouth of Tiny Lund during the Daytona 500. **5.** Rim-riding Mario Andretti races Jerry Grant (#40) and Henley Gray (#97) during the Daytona 500. Andretti found his car so loose he adopted an unorthodox line that left many of his rivals uncomfortable. **6.** The Holman-Moody crew services Mario Andretti's Ford during the Daytona 500. Andretti felt his crew held him on his final stop to allow teammate Fred Lorenzen to take the lead. Regardless, the 1966 Indianapolis 500 pole winner and future Formula One world champion led the final 33 laps to score an upset victory. **7.** With two laps remaining, Richard Petty blew his engine while running seventh in the #43 Plymouth, causing the Daytona 500 to finish under caution. Despite the quiet showing at Daytona, Petty earned the nickname "King Richard" with his greatest season, winning 27 of 48 races, including 10 in a row. Neither record has ever been challenged. **8.** Italian-born Mario Andretti enjoys his victory in the 1967 Daytona 500. His only triumph in a handful of NASCAR starts, Andretti went on to establish himself as one of the greatest drivers in history.

6.

7.

8.

Mario
Andretti #11 Ford

2. Fred Lorenzen   Ford
3. James Hylton   Dodge
4. Tiny Lund   Plymouth
5. Jerry Grant   Plymouth
6. Darel Dieringer   Ford
7. Sonny Hutchins   Ford
8. Richard Petty   Plymouth
9. Jim Hurtubise   Plymouth
10. Neil Castles   Plymouth

100-Mile Qualifying Race winners:
LeeRoy Yarbrough, Fred Lorenzen

1968

1.

1. Al Unser, driving the #6 Cotton Owens Dodge, races side-by-side with Paul Goldsmith in the #99 Nichels Engineering Plymouth during the 1968 Daytona 500. Cars giving chase include Sam McQuagg in the #37 K&K Dodge, Bobby Isaac in the #71 K&K Dodge, Bud Moore in the #1 Activated Angels Dodge, and Buddy Baker in the #3 Ray Fox Dodge. Unser, a future four-time winner of the Indianapolis 500, finished fourth in a rare NASCAR appearance. 2. David Pearson finished fifth in the 1968 Daytona 500 driving the #17 Holman-Moody Ford he raced to the 1968 championship. It was his second career title and his first of two consecutive crowns for Holman-Moody. 3. Yarborough vs. Yarbrough? Cale Yarborough, driving the #21 Wood Brothers Mercury, leads the #26 Junior Johnson Mercury driven by LeeRoy Yarbrough. While Yarbrough led six times for 62 laps, Yarborough overcame a late-race deficit to take the lead with four laps remaining. He gave the Wood Brothers their second Daytona 500 victory by a margin of one second. 4. Buddy Baker led the race three times in the #3 Ray Fox Dodge before being taken out in an accident that also involved defending race winner Mario Andretti. 5. Bud Moore, driving the #1 Dodge, loses control in the first turn in three-wide action. Both he and James Hylton in the #48 Dodge were taken out in the mishap. USAC Champion Butch Hartman, making his first NASCAR start, gets by in the #5 Dodge and finishes 16th.

2.

3.

4.

5.

6.

6. Richard Petty competed with a black vinyl roof on his #43 Petty Blue Plymouth. Why he did so is unknown, but the top peeled back during the race forcing an unscheduled pit stop. Petty went on to finish eighth. **7.** Cale Yarborough came from a lap down to win the 1968 Daytona 500 in the Wood Brothers #21 Mercury.

7.

Cale Yarborough
#21 Mercury

2. LeeRoy Yarbrough   Mercury
3. Bobby Allison   Ford
4. Al Unser   Dodge
5. David Pearson   Ford
6. Paul Goldsmith   Plymouth
7. Darel Dieringer   Dodge
8. Richard Petty   Plymouth
9. Tiny Lund   Mercury
10. Andy Hampton   Dodge

125-Mile Qualifying Race winners:
None; inclement weather.

1969

1.

2.

3.

4.

5.

1. Buddy Baker (right) holds the trophy for winning the pole position for the 1969 Daytona 500 in the Ray Fox-owned Dodge. While Baker quit his qualifying race after only two laps to save his car for the Daytona 500, Bobby Isaac (left), the second-fastest qualifier, raced his heat and won. **2.** Bobby Isaac accepts the trophy after winning the second qualifying race. This was the first year the twin qualifying races ran a 125-mile distance; NASCAR increased it after Fred Lorenzen won a 100-mile qualifier without stopping for fuel in 1967. The races were rained out in 1968. **3.** Unhappy with the lack of competitiveness of his car, Richard Petty (#43) switched to a Ford Torino in 1969 and finished eighth in the Daytona 500. He's shown trailing the #27 Banjo Matthews Ford of Donnie Allison. **4.** Eventual winner LeeRoy Yarbrough tackles one of Daytona's high-banked turns in Junior Johnson's #98 Ford. **5.** Cale Yarborough cut a tire and hit the Turn 4 wall in the #21 Wood Brothers Mercury. The defending champion led 17 laps in the early going. **6.** While "Charging Charlie" Glotzbach dominated the latter stages of the 1969 Daytona 500, he lost the lead on the final lap and finished second, one car length behind LeeRoy Yarbrough. **7.** LeeRoy Yarbrough, driving Junior Johnson's #98 Ford Torino, passes Charlie Glotzbach in Cotton Owens' #6 Dodge Charger on the final lap of the Daytona 500. Glotzbach attempted a slingshot pass but fell short. This was the first Daytona 500 to be determined by a last-lap pass. **8.** The Junior Johnson team welcomes LeeRoy Yarbrough in the makeshift Victory Lane in the Speedway tri-oval following the Daytona 500. **9.** LeeRoy Yarbrough wears a laurel wreath and holds the Cannonball Baker Trophy after winning the 1969 Daytona 500.

6.

7.

8.

9.

LeeRoy Yarbrough #98 Ford

2. Charlie Glotzbach   Dodge
3. Donnie Allison   Ford
4. A.J. Foyt   Ford
5. Buddy Baker   Dodge
6. David Pearson   Ford
7. Benny Parsons   Ford
8. Richard Petty   Ford
9. Andy Hampton   Dodge
10. Ray Elder   Dodge

125-Mile Qualifying Race winners:
David Pearson, Bobby Isaac

1970

1.

2.

3.

1. Cale Yarborough won the pole for the Daytona 500 with a record lap of 194.015 in the Wood Brothers Mercury, and then set a record in winning the first 125-mile Twin Qualifying Race at 183.295 mph. He beat eventual 1970 NASCAR champion Bobby Isaac's K&K Dodge Daytona by 5.5 seconds. **2.** One year after finishing a close second in the Daytona 500, Charlie Glotzbach won the second 125-mile Twin Qualifying Race. Driving Ray Nichel's winged Dodge Daytona, Glotzbach passed the Dodge of Buddy Baker with 14 laps remaining and won by 4.7 seconds. **3.** Talladega winner Richard Brickhouse, in the #14 Bill Ellis Plymouth Superbird, battles the #55 Dodge Daytona of Tiny Lund during the second qualifying race. Giving chase are Buddy Baker in the #6 Dodge Daytona and Bob Ashbrook, who failed to qualify in the #44 Chevrolet. Baker finished second behind winner Charlie Glotzbach, while Lund and Brickhouse finished fourth and fifth, respectively. **4.** While the winged #43 Plymouth Superbird remains one of Richard Petty's signature cars, teammate Pete Hamilton actually had greater success in his #40 Superbird. **5.** Bobby Allison had a strong Speedweeks in the #22 Dodge Daytona owned by Mario Rossi. He finished third in both his qualifying race and the Daytona 500. **6.** Nine of the new winged Chrysler cars were among the first 12 starters in the 1970 Daytona 500, with the Dodge Daytonas and Plymouth Superbirds attracting plenty of attention. Cale Yarborough managed to win the pole in a year-old Mercury fastback (#21) owned by the Wood Brothers. On the outside of the front row was Buddy Baker in

4.

5.

Cotton Owens' #6 Dodge Daytona. On the second row were Bobby Isaac in the #71 K&K Dodge and Charlie Glotzbach in the #99 Nichels-Goldsmith Dodge. Bobby Allison started sixth in Mario Rossi's #22 Dodge, while Tiny Lund rolled off eighth in the #55 Dodge. Eventual winner Pete Hamilton started ninth in the #40 Petty Enterprises Plymouth and was joined on the fifth row by Richard Brickhouse in the #14 Plymouth. On the sixth row were the Plymouth of Richard Petty and the Dodge of Ray Elder. Other Fords among the first six rows were Junior Johnson's #98 Torino driven by LeeRoy Yarbrough, starting fifth, and Donnie Allison, who started seventh in Banjo Matthews #27 Ford. **7.** While the winged cars caught the racing world's attention, a pair of year-old Ford fastbacks nearly took the big prize at the Daytona 500. Cale Yarborough won the pole and his qualifying race in the #21 Woods Brothers Mercury, shown leading the #55 Dodge Daytona of Tiny Lund. Yarborough dominated the early going before blowing his engine while leading after 31 laps. David Pearson went on to finish second in the Holman-Moody Ford, three car lengths behind winner Pete Hamilton. **8.** Pete Hamilton was king of the high-banked superspeedways in 1970. Driving the #40 Plymouth Superbird, Hamilton followed up his Daytona 500 triumph with victories in both races at Talladega Superspeedway.

6.

7.

8.

Pete Hamilton #40 Plymouth

2. David Pearson — Ford
3. Bobby Allison — Dodge
4. Charlie Glotzbach — Dodge
5. Bobby Isaac — Dodge
6. Richard Brickhouse — Plymouth
7. Jim Hurtubise — Ford
8. Ramo Stott — Plymouth
9. LeeRoy Yarbrough — Ford
10. Dave Marcis — Dodge

125-Mile Qualifying Race winners:
Cale Yarborough, Charlie Glotzbach

1971

1.

2.

3.

4.

1. Shown trailing the #18 Dodge of Joe Frasson, Fred Lorenzen brought STP sponsorship to his #99 Nichels-Goldsmith Plymouth for the 1971 Daytona 500. Ending a three-year retirement, Lorenzen finished fifth in both his qualifying race and the Daytona 500. **2.** One year after winning the NASCAR championship, Bobby Isaac returned in the #71 K&K Insurance Dodge. He led the Daytona 500 four times in the Harry Hyde-wrenched machine and went on to finish 10th. **3.** While NASCAR imposed strict engine requirements that all but ended the era of the winged stock cars, Mario Rossi entered the #22 Dodge Daytona with a small-block 305-cubic-inch engine driven by Dick Brooks, who led four times for five laps before spinning and losing two laps. He recovered to finish seventh. Brooks is shown racing the Mercurys of David Pearson (#17) and A.J. Foyt (#21), plus an unidentified Plymouth. **4.** Richard Petty's #43 Plymouth gets a push from his pit crew to get back in action in the 1971 Daytona 500. **5.** Dick Brooks lost out on his upset bid when his winged #22 Dodge Daytona spun near the halfway point and was hit by the #6 Cotton Owens Plymouth of Pete Hamilton. Eventual winner Richard Petty (#43) and fellow Plymouth driver Fred Lorenzen (#99), along with Bobby Allison in the #12 Dodge, get by on the outside. **6.** Buddy Baker, driving the #11 Dodge fielded by Petty Enterprises, leads the #6 Cotton Owens Plymouth of defending Daytona 500 winner Pete Hamilton. Baker finished second, 10 seconds behind teammate Richard Petty, while Hamilton won a qualifying race but blew his engine in the 500. **7.** 1971 would be the final time Richard Petty raced the Daytona 500 in a car without major sponsorship. He went on to win his third Daytona 500 in a Petty Blue Plymouth, defeating the Dodge of Petty Enterprises teammate Buddy Baker.

5.

6.

7.

Richard Petty #43 Plymouth

2. Buddy Baker — Dodge
3. A.J. Foyt — Mercury
4. David Pearson — Mercury
5. Fred Lorenzen — Plymouth
6. Jim Vandiver — Dodge
7. Dick Brooks — Dodge
8. Jim Hurtubise — Ford
9. James Hylton — Ford
10. Bobby Isaac — Dodge

125-Mile Qualifying Race winners:
Pete Hamilton, David Pearson

1972

1.

2.

3.

1. Bobby Allison (left) and Bobby Isaac kiss the trophy queen after winning the 125-mile qualifying races. **2.** Andy Granatelli (right) made headlines when it was announced that his company, STP Corp., purchased Petty Enterprises and would sponsor Richard Petty. **3.** A.J. Foyt, driving the #21 Wood Brothers Mercury, leads the #43 Plymouth of Richard Petty and the #12 Chevrolet of Bobby Allison during the 1972 Daytona 500. **4.** Roger Penske brought an AMC Matador to Daytona for 1971 Indianapolis 500 winner Mark Donohue. The pair were no strangers to Daytona, winning the 1969 24 Hours of Daytona while finishing third in 1971. Donohue finished fifth in his qualifying race but retired with engine problems and finished 35th in the Daytona 500.

4.

5.

5. If he wasn't in love with Indy Cars, A.J. Foyt might have become one of the greatest drivers in NASCAR history. The feisty Texan won seven NASCAR races, including the 1972 Daytona 500, where he piloted the Wood Brother's #21 Mercury to a one-lap victory. **6.** While A.J. Foyt won the Firecracker 400 twice, his only win in NASCAR's biggest race came in 1972. He had managed a third-place finish the previous year and finished fourth in '69. He would go on to another fourth-place finish in 1973, and run fifth in '74. **7.** Actor James Garner presents A.J. Foyt with the Governor's Cup following the 1972 Daytona 500.

6.

7.

A.J. Foyt #21 Mercury

2. Charlie Glotzbach   Dodge
3. Jim Vandiver   Dodge
4. Benny Parsons   Mercury
5. James Hylton   Ford
6. Cale Yarborough   Plymouth
7. David Sisco   Chevrolet
8. Jabe Thomas   Plymouth
9. John Sears   Plymouth
10. Vic Elford   Plymouth

125-Mile Qualifying Race winners:
Bobby Isaac, Bobby Allison

1973

1.

3.

2.

4.

1. Coo Coo Marlin (left) and Buddy Baker hold their trophies after winning their respective Twin 125-mile qualifying races. **2.** A pack of independent drivers battle during the second qualifying race. Charlie Roberts, driving the #77 Ford, leads the #61 Chevrolet of Clarence Lovell, the #8 Mercury of Ed Negre, the #48 Mercury of James Hylton, the #52 Chevrolet of Canadian Earl Ross, the #18 Dodge of Joe Frasson, and the #30 Chevrolet of Ray Mayne. Hylton led the group with a fifth-place finish. **3.** Coo Coo Marlin, driving the #14 Cunningham-Kelly Chevrolet, leads pole winner Pete Hamilton, David Pearson, Jim Vandiver, Bobby Isaac, A.J. Foyt, and Hershel McGriff during his qualifying race. Marlin held on to win by 1.5 seconds over McGriff, scoring his lone NASCAR victory. **4.** Pole winner Buddy Baker led most of the Daytona 500 in the #71 Dodge, shown battling Cale Yarborough's #11 Chevrolet. Late in the race, fellow Dodge driver Richard Petty scrambled into contention. Petty assumed command on a light-ning-fast pit stop with a dozen laps remaining. Baker gradually whittled away at the lead, but his luck ran out when his engine blew with six laps to go. **5.** Future Daytona 500 winners Benny Parsons and Darrell Waltrip race side-by-side during the 1973 Daytona 500. Parsons finished 30th in the #72 L.G. DeWitt Chevrolet Monte Carlo that carried him to that year's NASCAR championship. Waltrip finished 12th in the #95 Mercury. Also pictured is the #17 Chevrolet of Bill Dennis.

5.

6. Cale Yarborough raced for Junior Johnson for the first time in the Daytona 500, starting third in the Richard Howard-owned #11 Chevrolet formerly driven by Bobby Allison. He led the race six times for 25 laps before exiting with a blown engine while running second. **7.** Richard Petty switched to a Dodge for the 1973 Daytona 500 and came through with his fourth triumph in the classic. While STP offered him a large sum of money to paint the car STP's day-glow red, Petty wanted to keep his signature Petty Blue. The compromise resulted in a unique paint scheme.

6.

7.

Richard Petty #43 Dodge

2. Bobby Isaac — Ford
3. Dick Brooks — Dodge
4. A.J. Foyt — Chevrolet
5. Hershel McGriff — Plymouth
6. Buddy Baker — Dodge
7. James Hylton — Mercury
8. Ramo Stott — Mercury
9. Buddy Arrington — Dodge
10. Vic Parsons — Mercury

125-Mile Qualifying Race winners:
Buddy Baker, Coo Coo Marlin

1974

1.

2.

3.

"I was running so good that I was beginning to feel sorry for Richard. Then, before I knew it, I was feeling more sorry for myself."

—Donnie Allison

4.

1. The crippled #16 AMC Matador of Gary Bettenhausen is towed following a crash during the second qualifying race. Bettenhausen rebounded in the Roger Penske entry to finish 12th in the Daytona 500. On the banking, #43 Richard Petty leads the similar #31 Dodge Charger of Jim Vandiver. While Petty went out with engine problems, Vandiver finished second in the qualifying race behind Cale Yarborough. **2.** Brothers Maurice (left) and Richard Petty (right) meet with NASCAR President Bill France in the NASCAR garage. **3.** Pole winner David Pearson, driving the #21 Wood Brothers Mercury, and Richard Petty, in the #43 STP Dodge, lead the field to the start of the Daytona 500. Officially, however, the green flag marked the beginning of the 21st circuit. The race distance was shortened to 450 miles due to the gas shortage. As a result, the first 20 laps were not scored so the race would remain a 500 miler. **4.** Eventual winner Richard Petty, in the #43 Dodge, gets the jump on the #11 Chevrolet of Cale Yarborough. Pole sitter David Pearson did not get a great start in the #21 Wood Brothers Mercury, causing Bobby Isaac, George Follmer, and Donnie Allison—who is all the way down on the apron in the #88 DiGard Chevrolet—to scramble to the inside. **5.** Donnie Allison in the #88 DiGard Chevrolet leads the #43 STP Dodge of Richard Petty in the late stages of the Daytona 500. Allison cut a tire and spun with 11 laps to go. **6.** While Donnie Allison and Richard Petty both hit debris late in the race, Petty was able to take his #43 STP Dodge to the pits for service when he cut a tire with 19 laps remaining. Allison held a big lead but had already passed the pit entrance when he cut his tires with 11 laps left, causing him to lose a lap and finish sixth. **7.** Coo Coo Marlin in the #14 Chevrolet was in a position to win the 1974 Daytona 500 before being black flagged for a potential loose lug nut. Marlin was leading a pack of three cars running just ahead of Richard Petty at the tail end of the lead lap when Petty took the checkered flag. When Marlin saw the checkered flag, he slowed down, falling from second to fourth in the final standings. "I thought I had won the race," explained a disappointed Marlin.

5.

6.

7.

Richard Petty #43 Dodge

2.	Cale Yarborough	Chevrolet
3.	Ramo Stott	Chevrolet
4.	Coo Coo Marlin	Chevrolet
5.	A.J. Foyt	Chevrolet
6.	Donnie Allison	Chevrolet
7.	Darrell Waltrip	Chevrolet
8.	Bobby Isaac	Chevrolet
9.	Dick Brooks	Dodge
10.	Walter Ballard	Chevrolet

125-Mile Qualifying Race winners:
Bobby Isaac, Cale Yarborough

1975

1.

3.

2.

4.

1. David Pearson in the #21 Wood Brothers Mercury and Richard Petty's #43 STP Dodge line up in the front row for the second qualifying race. The pair finished in that order. Both of the second-row starters, Ramo Stott in the #83 Chevrolet and Darrell Waltrip in the #17 Chevrolet, went out early with engine problems. **2.** Randy Tissott, driving the #74 Charles Little Chevrolet, drops to the inside to avoid an incident involving the #99 Dodge of Jim Vandiver, the #60 Chevrolet of Joe Mihalek, and the #75 Mercury of Dick Trickle. A short-track star from Wisconsin, Trickle would become NASCAR Raybestos Rookie of the Year in 1989. The fourth-lap crash eliminated nine of the 40 starters. **3.** Cars are lined up on pit road prior to the start of the 1975 Daytona 500. Donnie Allison won the pole in the #88 DiGard Chevrolet. In the second row are Bobby Allison, who won the first qualifying race in Roger Penske's #16 Matador, and Richard Petty in the #43 STP Dodge. **4.** Long before Jeff Gordon came to NASCAR, there was another Gordon driving a #24 Chevrolet. That was independent racer Cecil Gordon, shown racing the #48 Chevrolet of James Hylton in the Daytona 500. Gordon, who later became a crewman on Dale Earnhardt's championship team, finished 15th. Hylton, who finished third in the 1975 championship, placed 10th. **5.** Junior Johnson, Daytona 500 winner as both a driver (1960) and car owner (1969), fielded the car that finished third in 1975 with Cale Yarborough at the wheel. **6.** Eventual winner Benny Parsons (#72) races Darrell Waltrip (#17) in a battle of Chevrolet Lagunas. Waltrip went on to finish 26th. **7.** Ramo Stott, an inde-

> ## "This is the biggest day of my life—better than winning the championship."
> —Benny Parsons

5.

6.

pendent racer from Keokuk, Iowa, finished fifth in the Daytona 500 driving the #83 Chevrolet. He's shown racing Coo Coo Marlin, whose #14 Chevrolet suffered engine problems and finished 17th. **8.** Benny Parsons scored the biggest victory of his career, driving the #72 King's Row Fireplace Shops Chevrolet owned by L.G. DeWitt. Parsons, who started 32nd, used the draft of Richard Petty's overheating Dodge to get back into contention. When race leader David Pearson spun with less than three laps remaining, Parsons scored a dramatic victory, beating Bobby Allison by more than a lap.

7.

8.

Benny Parsons #72 Chevrolet

2.	Bobby Allison	Matador
3.	Cale Yarborough	Chevrolet
4.	David Pearson	Mercury
5.	Ramo Stott	Chevrolet
6.	Dave Marcis	Dodge
7.	Richard Petty	Dodge
8.	Richie Panch	Chevrolet
9.	G.C. Spencer	Dodge
10.	James Hylton	Chevrolet

125-Mile Qualifying Race winners:
Bobby Allison, David Pearson

1976

1.

2.

3.

1. During Pole Day qualifying for the 1976 Daytona 500, A.J. Foyt was fastest with a speed of 187.477 mph in Hoss Ellington's #28 Chevrolet; he's shown running beside the #83 Chevrolet of Ramo Stott. However, aside from similarly quick laps by Darrell Waltrip and Dave Marcis, virtually all the other contenders were 8 to 10 mph off the pace. The wide discrepancy caused NASCAR officials to reinspect the top three qualifiers. The cars of Foyt and Waltrip were found to have illegal nitrous-oxide bottles, and that of Marcis was disqualified for a radiator technicality. All three times were thrown out. **2.** Dave Marcis, driving the #71 K&K Dodge, duels with Buddy Baker in Bud Moore's #15 Ford during the first qualifying race. The pair battled side-by-side for several laps before Marcis prevailed in a near photo finish. **3.** Because of the strange turn of events in qualifying, the 1976 Daytona 500 had an unusual front row. Midwesterner Ramo Stott started on

4.

5.

the pole in the #83 Chevrolet, while Terry
Ryan started outside in the #81 Chevrolet.
4. Benny Parsons, driving the #72 King's
Row Chevrolet, leads the #11 Holly Farms
Chevrolet of Cale Yarborough. Parsons was
running third when the leaders tangled
on the last lap, and he finished third, one
lap down. Although Yarborough blew his
engine early and finished last, he went on
to capture his first NASCAR championship
for Junior Johnson. **5.** David Pearson had
the Wood Brothers #21 Purolator Mercury
in the lead nine times for 37 laps, including the final circuit. He's shown leading the
#43 Dodge of Richard Petty, the #2 Penske
Racing Mercury of Bobby Allison, and the
#72 Chevrolet of Benny Parsons. On the
inside is the #52 Chevrolet of Earl Ross.
6. David Pearson, Purolator, and a #21
Mercury were a consistent and successful
combination during most of the 1970s.
7. Number 21 David Pearson and #43
Richard Petty fly nose-to-tail in the closing
laps of the 1976 Daytona 500. On the final
lap, the two superstars got together for an
unforgettable finish.

6.

7.

1976

1.

> "At least me and David did our thing in front of the grandstands so all the people could see it. It must have been quite a finish from their standpoint."
>
> —Richard Petty

2.

3.

4.

5.

6.

7.

Richard Petty took the white flag for the Daytona 500 in the #43 STP Dodge with David Pearson's #21 Purolator Mercury on his back bumper, poised for a last-lap slingshot. Pearson made his move on the backstretch, taking the lead in Turn 3 with slight contact between the two. Petty pulled alongside Pearson in Turn 4. The two bumped again as Petty lurched into the lead. **1.** The bump sends Pearson's #21 Mercury spinning toward the grass. Petty keeps control of his #43 Dodge a moment longer, then slams headfirst into the wall. **2.** While Petty bounces off the wall, Pearson is tagged by the #18 Chevrolet of Joe Frasson, who had ducked onto the pit road entrance trying to avoid the melee. **3.** Petty spins into the grass. **4.** Meanwhile, Frasson and Pearson slide past pit road. Pearson had the presence of mind to disengage the clutch during his spin, thus keeping his engine running. **5-7.** Pearson makes his way through the grass past Frasson and then Petty, whose car came to rest only 100 feet from the finish line. Pearson's mangled Mercury took the checkered flag at 20 mph. **8.** Petty's crew runs to the grass to push their crippled car to the finish. The assistance was illegal, although Petty maintained his second-place finish, one lap down.

8.

David Pearson #21 Mercury

2. Richard Petty — Dodge
3. Benny Parsons — Chevrolet
4. Lennie Pond — Chevrolet
5. Neil Bonnett — Chevrolet
6. Terry Ryan — Chevrolet
7. J.D. McDuffie — Chevrolet
8. Terry Bivins — Chevrolet
9. Richard Childress — Chevrolet
10. Frank Warren — Dodge

125-Mile Qualifying Race winners:
Dave Marcis, Darrell Waltrip

1977

1.

2.

3.

4.

1. Number 1 Donnie Allison and #51 A.J. Foyt led the field to the green flag for the start of the 1977 Daytona 500. Allison won the pole with a lap of 188.048 mph in Hoss Ellington's Chevrolet, with Foyt fielding his own Chevrolet. Richard Petty and Cale Yarborough were scheduled to start on the second row after winning their qualifying races, but Petty pitted on the parade lap with an oil leak, moving #21 David Pearson up to third for the green flag. **2.** The men who emerged victorious in America's two biggest races of 1977 chat at Daytona. Cale Yarborough (left) went on to win the Daytona 500, with A.J. Foyt sixth in the stock car classic. Foyt went on to win an unprecedented fourth Indianapolis 500 in May. **3.** Pioneering female driver Janet Guthrie talks with Cale Yarborough in the NASCAR garage. After failing to make the 1976 Indianapolis 500, a Charlotte Motor Speedway promoter urged area businessperson Linda Ferreri to purchase a stock car from Hoss Ellington for Guthrie to drive in the World 600. Guthrie earned the respect of her competitors by finishing 15th in that event, placing 12th in the 1977 Daytona 500 and adding four top-10 finishes by the end of the year.

5.

4. Number 11 Cale Yarborough leads #43 Richard Petty during the Daytona 500. Petty started last after pitting on the parade lap with an oil leak. He worked his way back into contention before a blown engine took him out after 111 laps. **5.** Cale Yarborough, driving Junior Johnson's #11 Holly Farms Chevrolet Lumina S-3, leads the #43 Dodge of Richard Petty and the #21 Mercury of David Pearson in the Daytona 500. Yarborough scored his second victory in the event, while his rivals both went out with blown engines. **6.** Cale Yarborough enjoyed an incredible 1977 season in the #11 Chevrolet. He racked up a total of nine wins, scored 25 top-five finishes, finished in the top 10 in all but three of the 30 races, and was running at the finish of every event.

6.

Cale Yarborough

#11 Chevrolet

2.	Benny Parsons	Chevrolet
3.	Buddy Baker	Ford
4.	Coo Coo Marlin	Chevrolet
5.	Dick Brooks	Ford
6.	A.J. Foyt	Chevrolet
7.	Darrell Waltrip	Chevrolet
8.	Jimmy Means	Chevrolet
9.	Bob Burcham	Chevrolet
10.	James Hylton	Chevrolet

125-Mile Qualifying Race winners:
Richard Petty, Cale Yarborough

1978

1.

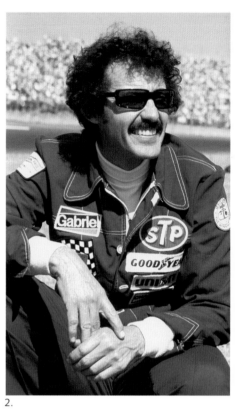

2.

3.

4.

5.

1. Bobby Allison's Speedweeks got off to a rough start in the opening Twin 125-mile Qualifying Race when his #15 Bud Moore Ford tangled with the #27 M.C. Anderson Oldsmobile of Buddy Baker. Getting around are Cale Yarborough in the #11 Oldsmobile and David Pearson in his familiar #21 Mercury. **2.** Richard Petty was smiling at the start of 1978, looking forward to racing what he thought was a sleek Dodge Magnum. However, the car didn't live up to his expectations, leading Petty to switch to General Motors by mid-year. Petty had a winless season, finishing sixth in the point standings. **3.** Cale Yarborough (#11) works to the outside of Bobby Allison's Ford (#15) during the Daytona 500. Switching to an Oldsmobile and Citicorp sponsorship for Junior Johnson, Yarborough won 10 races and an unprecedented third consecutive NASCAR title. **4.** The top three cars had broken from the pack by lap 60, when Richard Petty cut a tire on his #43 STP Dodge Magnum, taking himself out along with the #88 DiGard Chevrolet of Darrell Waltrip and the #21 Wood Brothers Mercury of David Pearson. **5.** Racing three-wide in the Daytona 500 are A.J. Foyt in his #51 Valvoline Buick, Cale Yarborough in Junior Johnson's #11 Citicorp Oldsmobile, and Buddy Baker in M.C. Anderson's #27 Oldsmobile. With the Dodge Charger and Chevrolet Laguna obsolete, many of the teams switched models. **6.** Bobby Allison switched to Bud Moore's Ford team, winning five races—including the Daytona 500— and finishing second in the championship standings.

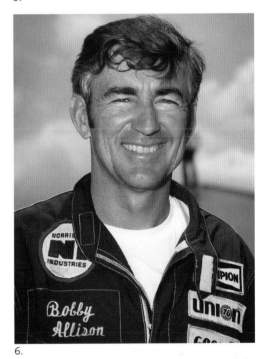

6.

Bobby Allison #15 Ford

2.	Cale Yarborough	Oldsmobile
3.	Benny Parsons	Oldsmobile
4.	Ron Hutcherson	Buick
5.	Dick Brooks	Mercury
6.	Dave Marcis	Chevrolet
7.	Buddy Baker	Oldsmobile
8.	Bill Elliott	Mercury
9.	Ferrell Harris	Dodge
10.	Lenny Pond	Oldsmobile

125-Mile Qualifying Race winners:
A.J. Foyt, Darrell Waltrip

1979

1.

2.

3.

4.

1. Buddy Baker (left) brought a lot of momentum into the 1979 Daytona 500. After winning the pole position with a lap of 196.049 mph, he led all but two laps and held off Darrell Waltrip to win the inaugural Busch Clash, a 20-lap sprint for pole winners from the previous year. He then joined Waltrip in winning the Twin 125-mile qualifying races. Baker is shown with his Busch Clash trophy. 2. Lennie Pond crashes in the #54 Oldsmobile while Geoffrey Bodine takes to the grass in the #47 Oldsmobile during the second Twin 125-Mile Qualifying Race. Avoiding the incident are Dave Marcis in the #02 Chevrolet and Dick Brooks in the #05 Oldsmobile. 3. NASCAR's stellar group of rookies in 1979 included (from left) Joe Milliken, Dale Earnhardt, and Terry Labonte. Harry Gant, Geoffrey Bodine, and Dave Watson were other notable rookies. Earnhardt, Bodine, and Watson went on to lead that year's Daytona 500. 4. Dale Earnhardt (right) talks with car owner Rod Osterlund. Driving the #2 Buick, Earnhardt finished fourth in his qualifying race and led the Daytona 500 five times for 10 laps before finishing eighth. 5. Donnie Allison in the #1 Oldsmobile takes the lead at the drop of the green flag in the 1979 Daytona 500. Buddy Baker in the #28 Oldsmobile led the opening 15 laps under caution, but his car misfired and the pole winner retired after only 38 laps. 6. Darrell Waltrip, driving DiGard's #88 Gatorade Oldsmobile, leads a group of cars including Tighe Scott's #30 Buick and Bobby Allison's #15 Ford. 7. Buddy Baker, in Harry Ranier's #28 Oldsmobile, leads the #05 Oldsmobile of Dick Brooks, the #2 Buick of Dale Earnhardt, the #47 Oldsmobile of Geoffrey Bodine, the #51 Oldsmobile of A.J. Foyt, the #02 Chevrolet of Dave Marcis, and the #12 Oldsmobile of Harry Gant. 8. While Donnie Allison in the #1 Oldsmobile and Cale Yarborough in the #11 Oldsmobile dominated the finish of the 1979 Daytona 500, rookie Dale Earnhardt in the #2 Buick stayed up front for much of the race before finishing eighth. 9. Donnie Allison's #1 Hawaiian Tropic Oldsmobile is serviced by the Hoss Ellington pit crew.

5.

6.

7.

8.

9.

1979: The 21st Annual Daytona 500 **55**

1.

2.

> "I made up my mind that if he was going to pass me, he would have to pass me high. When he tried to pass me low, he went off the track. He spun and hit me."
>
> —Donnie Allison

1. For the first time, the Daytona 500 was broadcast live, flag-to-flag, to a national television audience. Helping boost the CBS audience was the fact that the northeastern United States was blanketed in snow. The race earned a 10.5 Nielsen rating, but the rating jumped to 13.5 for the final half-hour. At the white flag, Donnie Allison (#1) led Cale Yarborough (#11) as the two Oldsmobiles broke away from the pack and were set to settle it on the final lap. **2.** Exiting Turn 2, Cale Yarborough ducked to the inside to attempt a slingshot pass. Allison went lower and lower to protect the low line. Yarborough went to the grass and then came back into the car of Allison—sending both into the wall. **3.** After they climbed from their cars, Yarborough (center) and Allison (right) got into a heated discussion. **4.** Richard Petty (#43) beats Darrell Waltrip (#88) to the checkered flag. A.J. Foyt (#51), who slowed momentarily when the caution was displayed, took third. Fourth in line was Tighe Scott in Walter Ballard's #30 Buick. Scott had held his own with the leaders throughout the race and was running third entering his final pit stop. He hit a puddle on pit road, overshot his pit, and lost a lap. Knowing he was a lap down, he moved over to allow Foyt, Petty, and Waltrip to get by on the final lap. Scott finished sixth, behind the lead trio and the wrecked cars of Allison and Yarborough.

3.

4.

5.

6.

5. The backstretch drama intensified when Bobby Allison pulled over to "check on his brother's condition." Yarborough and Bobby Allison then engaged in fisticuffs while a safety worker pulled Donnie Allison away. **6.** Bobby Allison attempts to tackle Yarborough moments before their brief scuffle was broken up. "For some reason, Cale kept hitting my fist repeatedly with his nose," Allison later explained. Yarborough, however, appeared to have held his own. While NASCAR put all three drivers on probation, the fight made great television and helped increase the public's interest in NASCAR. **7.** Richard Petty's crew hops aboard the #43 STP Oldsmobile for a ride to Victory Lane.

7.

Richard Petty #43 Oldsmobile

2.	Darrell Waltrip	Oldsmobile
3.	A.J. Foyt	Oldsmobile
4.	Donnie Allison	Oldsmobile
5.	Cale Yarborough	Oldsmobile
6.	Tighe Scott	Buick
7.	Chuck Bown	Buick
8.	Dale Earnhardt	Buick
9.	Coo Coo Marlin	Chevrolet
10.	Frank Warren	Dodge

125-Mile Qualifying Race winners:
Buddy Baker, Darrell Waltrip

1980

1.

2.

3.

1. Dale Earnhardt celebrated his first victory at Daytona International Speed-way when he won the second annual Busch Clash. He then finished fourth in the Daytona 500. Running in only his second full season, Earnhardt went on to capture the NASCAR championship for Rod Osterlund. He is shown with his future wife, Teresa Houston. **2.** After winning the pole with a lap of 194.009 mph, Buddy Baker in the #28 Oldsmobile led 143 laps to win the Daytona 500. **3.** Driving the #28 Oldsmobile, Buddy Baker's biggest rival proved to be sophomore driver Dale Earnhardt in the #2 Oldsmobile, who led 10 laps. "He was fast, but so was I," Earnhardt said. Baker passed Earnhardt to take the lead for keeps on lap 182 and won by 12 seconds over Bobby Allison. **4.** After years of trying, Buddy Baker finally won the Daytona 500—and did it in dominating fashion. **5.** The Harry Ranier pit crew and well-wishers surround Buddy Baker's winning #28 Oldsmobile in Victory Lane following the "Gentle Giant's" record-breaking performance. **6.** While Buddy Baker won 19 NASCAR races, none was bigger than the 1980 Daytona 500. His average speed of 177.602 mph remains the event record.

4.

5.

6.

"I've been trying to win this race for nearly 20 years. When a car runs that well, all I had to do was keep it between the walls. No one could touch me today. Waddell Wilson [Baker's crew chief] is the true reason I won today."

—Buddy Baker

Buddy Baker #28 Oldsmobile

2. Bobby Allison — Ford
3. Neil Bonnett — Mercury
4. Dale Earnhardt — Oldsmobile
5. Benny Parsons — Oldsmobile
6. Terry Labonte — Oldsmobile
7. Donnie Allison — Oldsmobile
8. Sterling Marlin — Chevrolet
9. Lennie Pond — Buick
10. Jody Ridley — Mercury

125-Mile Qualifying Race winners:
Neil Bonnett, Donnie Allison

1981

1.

1. Bobby Allison, driving Harry Ranier's #28 Pontiac LeMans, and Darrell Waltrip, in Junior Johnson's #11 Mountain Dew Buick, lead the field to the green flag in the 1981 Daytona 500. Allison won the pole and Waltrip won the Busch Clash, with both drivers taking their 125-mile qualifying race. Back in eighth for the start is Richard Petty, who had been overlooked in the Petty Enterprises #43 STP Buick. **2.** After missing his bid for a fourth NASCAR championship by 19 points to sophomore driver Dale Earnhardt in 1980, Cale Yarborough left Junior Johnson to drive a limited schedule for M.C. Anderson. He finished 15th in his qualifying race and eighth in the Daytona 500. **3.** Darrell Waltrip bought out his contract with DiGard to join Junior Johnson. He dropped out of the Daytona 500 on lap 117 with engine problems but went on to win 12 races and the 1981 NASCAR championship. **4.** Seen here trailing Bobby Allison in Harry Ranier's #28 Pontiac LeMans, Richard Petty used pit strategy to win his seventh Daytona 500. After Allison and the other leaders took on tires during their final green-flag pit stops, Petty took gas only and was able to beat Allison to the checkered flag by 3.5 seconds.

2.

3.

4.

5.

6.

5. Richard Petty takes the checkered flag after leading the final 25 laps for his seventh Daytona 500 triumph. A gas-and-go pit stop proved to be the key for Petty. Bobby Allison dominated the race, leading 117 laps in Harry Ranier's Pontiac, but Petty elected to take on gas only during his final stop. He moved from fifth to first on the last round of pit stops.
6. A pair of Daytona 500 winners bookend Linda Vaughn in Victory Lane. Lee Petty (left) won the inaugural Daytona 500, while his son's 1981 triumph was his seventh—and final—victory in the classic.

Richard Petty #43 Buick

2. Bobby Allison	Pontiac
3. Ricky Rudd	Oldsmobile
4. Buddy Baker	Oldsmobile
5. Dale Earnhardt	Pontiac
6. Bill Elliott	Ford
7. Jody Ridley	Ford
8. Cale Yarborough	Oldsmobile
9. Joe Millikan	Buick
10. Johnny Rutherford	Pontiac

125-Mile Qualifying Race winners:
Bobby Allison, Darrell Waltrip

1982

1.

1. Ron Bouchard, driving the #47 Race Hill Farms Buick, spins behind the #21 Wood Brothers Ford of Neil Bonnett during the second Twin 125-mile qualifying race. Avoiding the incident are the #42 STP Pontiac of Kyle Petty (Richard's son) and the #33 Mach 1 Racing Skoal Bandit Buick of Harry Gant. Bouchard recovered to finish 11th in the race won by Buddy Baker.
2. Benny Parsons gave Harry Ranier's #28 Pontiac its second consecutive Daytona 500 pole with a lap of 196.317 mph. His car was one of several sponsored by J.D. Stacy in the event. Harry Gant started on the outside of the front row in the #33 Skoal Bandit Buick, co-owned by Hollywood stuntman Hal Needham and actor Burt Reynolds. For the first time, the Daytona 500 opened the NASCAR season after running the opener on the road circuit at Riverside, California, for several years. **3.** Ploy or accident? Bobby Allison's DiGard #88 Gatorade Buick shed its rear bumper after being tagged by Cale Yarborough on the fourth lap, triggering a multi-car accident. After the incident, Allison dominated on the way to his second Daytona 500 victory. Looking in his rear-view mirror, he can see Dale Earnhardt in Bud Moore's #15 Ford, the Buicks of Buddy Baker (#1) and Darrell Waltrip (#11), and the #28 Pontiac of Benny Parsons. **4.** Bobby Allison, driving the #88 Gatorade Buick, leads the #15 Ford of Dale Earnhardt and the Buicks of Cale Yarborough (#27), Buddy Baker (#1), Harry Gant (#33), Terry Labonte (#44), and Darrell Waltrip (#11). Labonte finished fourth in a J.D. Stacy-sponsored entry for Billy Hagen.

"Allison cut me off. Suddenly his bumper came off. It didn't take much of a lick to tear it off."

—Cale Yarborough

2.

3.

4.

5. While Darrell Waltrip (right) had yet to share in Junior Johnson's success in the Daytona 500, the combination produced their second consecutive NASCAR championship in 1982. Waltrip blew an engine and finished 20th in the Daytona 500 but went on to win 12 races en route to Johnson's fifth title in seven years. **6.** Bobby Allison was a winner the first time out in the #88 DiGard Gatorade Buick. Daytona was the first of eight triumphs for the 44-year-old veteran, who finished second in the final NASCAR championship standings.

5.

6.

Bobby Allison #88 Buick

2. Cale Yarborough   Buick
3. Joe Ruttman   Buick
4. Terry Labonte   Buick
5. Bill Elliott   Ford
6. Ron Bouchard   Buick
7. Harry Gant   Buick
8. Buddy Baker   Buick
9. Jody Ridley   Ford
10. Roy Smith   Pontiac

125-Mile Qualifying Race winners:
Cale Yarborough, Buddy Baker

1983

1.

1. After running a record lap of 200.503 mph in qualifying for the Daytona 500, Cale Yarborough lost control of Harry Ranier's #28 Hardee's Pontiac and destroyed the car after bouncing off the Turn 4 wall and getting airborne. Yarborough went to a backup car and went on to win his third Daytona 500. 2. Dale Earnhardt (center), joined by his wife, Teresa, and car owner, Bud Moore, walks from Victory Lane after winning the opening Twin 125-Mile Qualifying Race. It was his first of 12 career triumphs in the non-championship event. 3. When Cale Yarborough's primary Pontiac was withdrawn after his qualifying crash, Ricky Rudd inherited the pole for the Daytona 500 after turning a lap of 198.864 mph in Richard Childress' #3 Piedmont Chevrolet. He was joined on the outside row by Geoffrey Bodine, who carried Gatorade sponsorship on Cliff Stewart's #88 Pontiac. Directly behind Rudd is Dale Earnhardt, carrying the Wrangler colors on Bud Moore's #15 Ford Thunderbird. 4. As the starting field runs down the frontstretch on the pace lap for the 1983 Daytona 500, the cars pass the race control booth that's perched atop the grandstand. The press box and suites are behind the glass windows at the back of the grandstands. Within a few years, the speedway would begin a mammoth transformation that would allow nearly double the crowd of 115,000 that saw the 1983 race. 5. Cale Yarborough (#28) leads the #43 STP Pontiac of Richard Petty during the Daytona 500. Yarborough went on to win, but Petty had a very strong run in quest of an eighth victory in the event. He started sixth and led four times for 29 laps. He lost his

2.

3.

4.

5.

engine while leading after 47 laps. **6.** Now bitter rivals after finishing 1-2 in the two most recent NASCAR championships, Darrell Waltrip—driving Junior Johnson's #11 Pepsi Challenger Chevrolet—leads Bobby Allison in the DiGard #22 Miller High Life Chevrolet. Waltrip was eliminated from the Daytona 500 in a crash on lap 63. Bobby Allison wrecked two cars during Speedweeks preliminaries and came back to finish ninth. The pair finished 1-2 in the 1983 championship, with Allison winning his first title by 47 points.

6.

Cale Yarborough

#28 Pontiac

2.	Bill Elliott	Ford
3.	Buddy Baker	Ford
4.	Joe Ruttman	Chevrolet
5.	Dick Brooks	Ford
6.	Terry Labonte	Chevrolet
7.	Tom Sneva	Chevrolet
8.	David Pearson	Chevrolet
9.	Bobby Allison	Chevrolet
10.	Jody Ridley	Buick

125-Mile Qualifying Race winners:
Dale Earnhardt, Neil Bonnett

1984

1.

1-2. Ricky Rudd destroyed Bud Moore's #15 Ford Thunderbird in a spinning crash during the 1984 Busch Clash for 1983 pole winners. Rudd came back to finish seventh in both his qualifying race and the Daytona 500. The following week, the bruised warrior drove to victory at Richmond. 3. Junior Johnson rolled out a two-car team for 1984, with both of them carrying Budweiser sponsorship. Darrell Waltrip (right) returned to drive the #11 Chevrolet Monte Carlo, while Neil Bonnett drove the #12 machine. Waltrip and Bonnett finished third and fourth, respectively, in the Daytona 500. 4. Cale Yarborough (#28) leads the field through Turn 4 moments before the start of the 1984 Daytona 500. Joining him on the front row was Terry Labonte in Billy Hagen's #44 Piedmont Chevrolet, while up-and-comer Bill Elliott rolled off third in the #9 Melling Racing Coors Thunderbird. 5. Cale Yarborough captured the pole for the 1984 Daytona 500 after turning a lap of 201.848 mph in Harry Ranier's #28 Hardee's Chevrolet. He became Ranier's third driver in four years to win the Daytona 500 pole, following Bobby Allison and Benny Parsons. This does not include Yarborough's 200-mph fast lap in 1983, when he crashed and had to withdraw the car. 6. While Bobby Allison won a 125-mile qualifying race in the DiGard #22 Miller Buick, the defending NASCAR champion broke a camshaft in the Daytona 500 and finished 34th.

2.

3.

4.

5.

6.

1984

1.

1. Darrell Waltrip was one of six drivers battling for victory on the final lap of the 1984 Daytona 500. While he led at the white flag after leading 38 consecutive laps, Waltrip finished third in the last-lap scramble. He went on to score seven NASCAR victories in 1984 but slumped to fifth in the championship standings. **2.** Cale Yarborough in the #28 Hardee's Chevrolet held off Dale Earnhardt in the #3 Wrangler Chevrolet by eight car lengths to win his fourth—and final—Daytona 500. Yarborough won the race with a last-lap slingshot pass for the second straight year. Earnhardt returned to Richard Childress Racing, swapping the Bud Moore Ford Thunderbird with Ricky Rudd. Because Wrangler had strong ties to both Bud Moore and Dale Earnhardt, the company ended up sponsoring two cars in 1984. **3.** Terry Labonte had a strong showing in the Daytona 500. He started second in Billy Hagen's #44 Piedmont Chevrolet and was in contention until cutting a tire and scraping the wall with 10 laps remaining. He still finished 12th. Labonte went on to hold off Harry Gant to win the 1984 NASCAR championship. **4.** Crew chief Waddell Wilson (right) and the Ranier Racing crew join Cale Yarborough for the champagne spray following their Daytona 500 victory. After running second in a six-car train throughout the final 100 miles, Yarborough passed Darrell Waltrip in Turn 2 on the final lap and held off Dale Earnhardt for the victory.

2.

3.

> "I wanted to be in second place until the last lap. Once I got it, I held onto it until it was time to make my move."
>
> —Cale Yarborough

4.

Cale Yarborough

#28 Chevrolet

2. Dale Earnhardt   Chevrolet
3. Darrell Waltrip   Chevrolet
4. Neil Bonnett   Chevrolet
5. Bill Elliott   Ford
6. Harry Gant   Chevrolet
7. Ricky Rudd   Ford
8. Geoffrey Bodine   Chevrolet
9. David Pearson   Chevrolet
10. Jody Ridley   Chevrolet

125-Mile Qualifying Race winners:
Cale Yarborough, Bobby Allison

1985

1.

1. Three of the top contenders have their cars serviced on pit road. The Melling Racing team works on Bill Elliott's #9 Coors Ford, just ahead of the Hendrick Motorsports #5 Levi-Garrett Chevrolet of Geoffrey Bodine and Junior Johnson's #12 Chevrolet of Neil Bonnett. **2.** Lake Speed came to Daytona without a sponsor for the #75 RahMoc Pontiac. He's shown finishing seventh in the second Twin 125-mile qualifying race, won by Cale Yarborough. On the eve of the Daytona 500, Speed secured sponsorship from Nationwise Auto Parts and went on to score a heartwarming second-place finish. Yarborough, making a bid for a third-consecutive and fifth-career Daytona 500 victory, was a factor for the opening 150 miles before going out with a blown engine. **3.** Bill Elliott, driving the #9 Coors Ford Thunderbird, races to the inside of the #12 Budweiser Chevrolet Monte Carlo of Neil Bonnett. While Elliott dominated the race, Bonnett was his toughest contender. Bonnett led four times for 22 laps—all in the second half of the race—and was leading with six laps remaining when his engine blew. **4.** With "King Richard" driving for Curb Motorsports, his brother Maurice Petty and Petty Enterprises fielded the #1 Ford Thunderbird for Dick Brooks. He finished sixth in his qualifying race but retired from the Daytona 500 with a broken wheel. The team ceased operation in April but came back the following year with Petty's return to his team. **5.** A group of outsiders shocked the NASCAR world in 1985, when Dawsonville, Georgia-based Melling Racing—led by brothers Bill, Ernie, and Dan Elliott—dominated Speedweeks. Bill Elliott gets a quick pit stop during the Daytona 500 and went on to score a sweep of the pole, qualifying race, and Daytona 500.

2.

3.

4.

6. Bill Elliott in the #9 Ford takes the checkered flag to win the 1985 Daytona 500. He led 136 of the 200 laps after shattering the track record in qualifying with a speed of 205.114 mph. **7.** The Harley J. Earl Memorial Trophy was the first of many accolades for Bill Elliott in 1985. Before long, he earned the nickname "Awesome Bill From Dawsonville." Before the year was out, he was also called "Million Dollar Bill" after winning three of four designated major NASCAR races, for which he was awarded a million-dollar bonus from Series sponsor R.J. Reynolds.

5.

6.

7.

Bill Elliott #9 Ford

2.	Lake Speed	Pontiac
3.	Darrell Waltrip	Chevrolet
4.	Buddy Baker	Oldsmobile
5.	Ricky Rudd	Ford
6.	Greg Sacks	Chevrolet
7.	Geoffrey Bodine	Chevrolet
8.	Rusty Wallace	Pontiac
9.	Bobby Hillin Jr.	Chevrolet
10.	Neil Bonnett	Chevrolet

125-Mile Qualifying Race winners:
Bill Elliott, Cale Yarborough

1986

1.

2.

3.

4.

1. Dale Earnhardt (left) relaxes with A.J. Foyt prior to the Daytona 500. Earnhardt won his qualifying race and the Busch Clash before contending in the Daytona 500, when he ran out of gas and blew his engine while running second with three laps remaining. Foyt's luck was even worse; he went out with engine problems in his own Oldsmobile and finished 29th. **2.** Geoffrey Bodine, in the #5 Levi-Garrett Chevrolet, leads the field on a restart during the Daytona 500. In front on the inside row is Kyle Petty, who finished 16th in the #7 Wood Brothers 7-Eleven Ford. **3.** Tim Richmond leads a pack of cars in the Hendrick Motorsports #25 Folgers Chevrolet. He finished 20th in the Daytona 500. He is followed by Bobby Allison, who blew an engine and finished 42nd in his first drive for the Stavola Brothers in the #22 Miller Buick. Behind Allison is Bill Elliott, who won the pole with a lap of 205.039 mph and won a qualifying race in the Melling Racing #9 Coors Ford but was never a factor in the Daytona 500 and finished 13th. **4.** When Joe Ruttman broke a wheel on the King Racing #26 Quaker State Buick, it triggered a multi-car pileup. Neil Bonnett spins to the apron in the Junior Johnson #12 Budweiser Chevrolet. Managing to avoid the incident are Bobby Hillin Jr. in the Stavola Brothers #8 Miller Chevrolet and Lake Speed in the #75 RahMoc Pontiac. Hillin led the group with a fourth-place finish.

5.

5. The Daytona 500 came down to a battle between a pair of rivals, Geoffrey Bodine in the #5 Levi Garrett Chevrolet and Dale Earnhardt in the #3 Wrangler Chevrolet. The pair broke away from the field and were preparing for a late-race showdown when Earnhardt had to pit for fuel with three laps remaining. His engine blew while he was exiting the pits, resulting in a 14th-place finish. **6.** Geoffrey Bodine led the final 44 laps to win the 1986 Daytona 500, beating Terry Labonte by 11.26 seconds to score his biggest career victory.

6.

Geoffrey Bodine #5 Chevrolet

2. Terry Labonte   Oldsmobile
3. Darrell Waltrip   Chevrolet
4. Bobby Hillin Jr.   Chevrolet
5. Benny Parsons   Oldsmobile
6. Ron Bouchard   Pontiac
7. Rick Wilson   Oldsmobile
8. Rusty Wallace   Pontiac
9. Sterling Marlin   Chevrolet
10. Lake Speed   Pontiac

125-Mile Qualifying Race winners:
Bill Elliott, Dale Earnhardt

1987

1.

2.

1. He's "Awesome." Bill Elliott won the pole for the 1987 Daytona 500 with a record qualifying speed of 210.364 mph. Three months later, Elliott won the pole at Talladega Superspeedway with a lap of 212.809 mph. Both records still stand and will likely never be broken. Following a flip by Bobby Allison into the frontstretch catch fence during the 1987 race at Talladega, NASCAR mandated restrictor plates at its two fastest tracks to drastically reduce speeds. **2.** Davey Allison races Benny Parsons during the second 125-mile qualifying race. The second-generation Allison started the race from the pole after setting the second-fastest time in qualifying with Ranier-Lundy's then-unsponsored #28 Ford. Parsons joined Hendrick Motorsports to replace the ailing Tim Richmond, who missed the early part of the season. Parsons drove the #35 Folgers Chevrolet, as the team reserved its #25 Chevrolet for Richmond, who returned to racing later in the year. Parsons won the race over Bobby Allison, with Davey Allison finishing sixth. **3.** The green flag waves for the start of the 1987 edition of "The Great American Race." Bill Elliott (#9) is joined on the front row by rookie Davey Allison (#28). Ken Schrader (obscured behind Elliott in the #90 Ford) edged the pole sitter by one foot to win his qualifying race. Starting fifth, behind Schrader, is Darrell Waltrip in his first race in Rick Hendrick's #17 Tide Chevrolet. **4.** Chevrolet switched to a slope-backed version of its Monte Carlo SS for 1987. Two of the cars are shown in side-by-side competition with Dale Earnhardt in the #3 Wrangler entry fielded by Richard Childress and Terry Labonte in the Budweiser #11 from Junior Johnson's operation. Earnhardt managed a fifth-place finish in the Daytona 500, while Labonte ended up 18th. **5.** Davey Allison began his rookie season on the front row for the Daytona 500 by virtue of qualifying with the second-fastest speed. The younger Allison replaced Cale Yarborough in the Ranier-Lundy #28 Ford Thunderbird. Although Allison finished 27th in the Daytona 500, he went on to win two races during the season, along with

3.

4.

5.

the NASCAR Raybestos Rookie of the Year award. **6.** Bill Elliott takes the checkered flag in the #9 Ford to win the Daytona 500 for the second time. Geoffrey Bodine tried to stretch his fuel mileage for a second-consecutive victory in the event, but his tank ran dry with three laps remaining. Elliott then held off Benny Parsons by three car lengths for the victory.

6.

Bill Elliott #9 Ford

2. Benny Parsons   Chevrolet
3. Richard Petty   Pontiac
4. Buddy Baker   Oldsmobile
5. Dale Earnhardt   Chevrolet
6. Bobby Allison   Buick
7. Ken Schrader   Ford
8. Darrell Waltrip   Chevrolet
9. Ricky Rudd   Ford
10. Cale Yarborough   Oldsmobile

125-Mile Qualifying Race winners:
Ken Schrader, Benny Parsons

1988

1.

3.

4.

1. Dale Earnhardt opened Speedweeks by winning the Busch Clash for the third time. **2.** The legend and the legacy: While Davey Allison (left) prepared to start his second full season driving for Ranier Racing, Bobby Allison's career would be cut short by an accident only four months after winning the 1988 Daytona 500. **3.** Bobby Allison, driving the #12 Miller Buick for the Stavola Brothers, leads Dale Earnhardt (#3) during the Daytona 500. **4.** Davey Allison, in the Ranier Racing #28 Texaco Havoline Ford, races alongside Dale Jarrett in the #1 Buick fielded by Hoss Ellington. Jarrett went on to finish 16th in his first Daytona 500. Behind Allison is Terry Labonte, new driver of Junior Johnson's #11 Chevrolet. **5.** Part of the crowd of 140,000 watches as Bobby Allison (#12) leads Harry Gant (#33), Trevor Boys (#95), Neil Bonnett (#75), and Phil Parsons (#55) during the

5.

6.

7.

8.

9.

Daytona 500. **6-9.** Richard Petty (#43) was involved in a crash on the 106th lap of the Daytona 500. He was bumped by Phil Barkdoll into the path of A.J. Foyt, then launched into the air and flipped a dozen times. Spinning to a stop, Petty was then T-boned by Brett Bodine in Bud Moore's #15 Ford. Petty escaped the incident with a sprained ankle and torn ligaments, and finished third the following weekend at Richmond. **10.** One year after his electrifying pole and second victory in the Daytona 500, Bill Elliott was a non-factor in Harry Melling's #9 Coors Thunderbird. He started 31st, never led, and finished 12th. He went on to win the big prize, though, capturing the 1988 NASCAR title.

10.

1988

1.

"It was just great looking in the mirror and seeing someone who you think is the best among those coming up now. To know it's your son is really a special feeling that's hard to describe."

—Bobby Allison

2.

3.

4.

1. Rusty Wallace finished seventh in the Daytona 500, driving Raymond Beadle's #27 Kodiak Pontiac for Blue Max Racing. He went on to finish second in the NASCAR championship, losing by 24 points to Bill Elliott. 2. Father and son lead the field in the Daytona 500, with Bobby Allison (#12) followed by Davey (#28). 3. Bobby Allison crosses the finish line two car lengths ahead of his son, Davey, for a 1-2 Allison finish in the 1988 Daytona 500. 4. Bobby Allison poses with the Stavola Brothers #12 Miller High Life Buick he drove to victory in both a 125-mile qualifying race and the Daytona 500. 5. Bobby Allison showers his son, Davey, with some of his sponsor's product in Victory Lane. Having driven a car sponsored by Havoline, it's a good thing Davey didn't return the favor.

5.

Bobby Allison #12 Buick

2.	Davey Allison	Ford
3.	Phil Parsons	Oldsmobile
4.	Neil Bonnett	Pontiac
5.	Terry Labonte	Chevrolet
6.	Ken Schrader	Chevrolet
7.	Rusty Wallace	Pontiac
8.	Sterling Marlin	Oldsmobile
9.	Buddy Baker	Oldsmobile
10.	Dale Earnhardt	Chevrolet

125-Mile Qualifying Race winners:
Bobby Allison, Darrell Waltrip

1989

1.

2.

1. Darrell Waltrip, driving the Hendrick Motorsports #17 Tide Chevrolet, takes the lead from pole-sitting teammate Ken Schrader in the #25 Folgers Chevrolet at the start of the 1989 Daytona 500. Morgan Shepherd runs third in the RahMoc Racing #75 Valvoline Pontiac, next to Junior Johnson's #11 Budweiser Ford of Terry Labonte. **2.** Ricky Rudd gets new left-side tires during a pit stop for the #26 Quaker State Buick. He finished 19th. **3.** Darrell Waltrip's #17 Tide Chevrolet leads Dale Earnhardt in the #3 GM Goodwrench Chevrolet, Geoffrey Bodine in the #5 Levi Garrett Chevrolet, Phil Parsons in the #55 Skoal Oldsmobile, and Rick Wilson in the #4 Kodak Oldsmobile. All five drivers finished the Daytona 500 in the top eight. **4.** Davey Allison (#28) limps back to the pits—sans hood—after sliding into a dirt embankment and flipping following contact with Geoffrey Bodine on lap 23. He returned to the race and finished 25th, seven laps down. **5.** Crew chief Barry Dodson seems to be looking for help during a long pit stop for the Blue Max Racing #27 Kodiak Pontiac of Rusty Wallace. While Wallace finished 18th in the Daytona 500, he went on to edge Dale Earnhardt by 12 points to win his only NASCAR championship.

3.

4.

5.

6. Ken Schrader, driving the Harry Hyde-wrenched #25 Folgers Chevrolet for Hendrick Motorsports, dominated the 1989 Daytona 500. He led the most laps but lost the lead when he pitted for fuel with 11 laps remaining. Hendrick teammate Darrell Waltrip gambled on his fuel and won in the #17 Tide Chevrolet. **7.** "I finally did it!" An emotional Darrell Waltrip celebrates his 74th NASCAR victory—but his first in the Daytona 500.

6.

7.

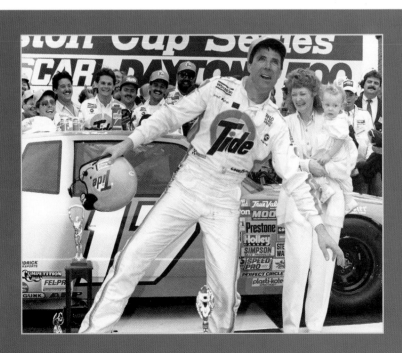

Darrell Waltrip #17 Chevrolet

2. Ken Schrader   Chevrolet
3. Dale Earnhardt   Chevrolet
4. Geoffrey Bodine   Chevrolet
5. Phil Parsons   Oldsmobile
6. Rick Mast   Chevrolet
7. Alan Kulwicki   Ford
8. Rick Wilson   Oldsmobile
9. Terry Labonte   Ford
10. Eddie Bierschwale   Oldsmobile

125-Mile Qualifying Race winners:
Ken Schrader, Terry Labonte

1990

1.

2.

3.

1. Dale Earnhardt (center) scored his third victory in a Twin 125-Mile Qualifying Race, passing Dick Trickle with three laps remaining and holding off Bill Elliott by less than half a second. Winning proved to be habit-forming for the Richard Childress Racing team. The celebration marked the first of 10 consecutive years that Earnhardt would win a Daytona qualifying race in the #3 GM Goodwrench Chevrolet. **2.** Geoffrey Bodine was a winner in his first race in Junior Johnson's #11 Budweiser Ford. Running the 125 miles without a pit stop, Bodine led the final two laps and beat Harry Gant to the checkered flag by two seconds. Bodine started the Daytona 500 from the pole when fast qualifier Ken Schrader moved to a backup car. **3.** Life imitates art: Greg Sacks, driving Rick Hendrick's #46 City Chevrolet, races to the high side of Daytona 500 pole winner and teammate Ken Schrader in the #25 Kodiak Chevrolet. Sacks was driving one of several cars prepared for the upcoming movie *Days of Thunder*. The cars were allowed to run in the early laps of the qualifying races and Daytona 500 but were not scored. Schrader crashed on the final lap, putting him in a backup car and sending him to the back of the grid for the Daytona 500. **4.** While he didn't compete in the Daytona 500, Tom Cruise—portraying the character Cole Trickle—spent time at Daytona taking advantage of the huge Speedweeks crowd to shoot scenes for the film *Days of Thunder*. **5.** Number 3 Dale Earnhardt dominated the 1990 Daytona 500. He led the race eight times for 154 laps, building up a 27-second lead at one point. He passed Derrike Cope and took the lead on a restart with five laps remaining. On the final lap, Earnhardt hit a piece of debris on the backstretch, cut a tire, and slowed. He managed to keep control, but finished fifth. **6.** Dale Earnhardt (#3) and Derrike Cope (#10) race side-by-side during the Daytona 500. While Earnhardt was the class of the field, Cope was the "best of the rest," taking advantage of Earnhardt's bad luck on the final lap to take the win. **7.** Derrike Cope (#10) takes the checkered flag to score the biggest upset in Daytona 500 history. Chasing him to the stripe are the #1 Oldsmobile of Terry Labonte and the #9 Ford of Bill Elliott.

4.

5.

6.

7.

"When you say you have a Daytona 500 win, that's like a Super Bowl ring. Obviously, winning the Daytona 500 is the biggest accomplishment in my career. When you win the Daytona 500, you have a very big place in history. It's always going to be there. No one could ever say I didn't accomplish something great with my life."

—Derrike Cope

Derrike Cope #10 Chevrolet

2. Terry Labonte   Oldsmobile
3. Bill Elliott   Ford
4. Ricky Rudd   Chevrolet
5. Dale Earnhardt   Chevrolet
6. Bobby Hillin Jr.   Buick
7. Rusty Wallace   Pontiac
8. Michael Waltrip   Pontiac
9. Geoffrey Bodine   Ford
10. Morgan Shepherd   Ford

125-Mile Qualifying Race winners:
Geoffrey Bodine, Dale Earnhardt

1991

1.

2.

1. Dale Earnhardt (middle of back row) celebrates with his crew after winning the second Gatorade Twin 125-Mile Qualifying Race. **2.** Sponsorless after losing Zerex as a sponsor, Alan Kulwicki carried Army colors in the Daytona 500. In a display of unity during Operation Desert Shield and the impending invasion of Iraq by U.S. troops, five of the cars competing in the Daytona 500 were painted in the colors of the Armed Forces. Other cars were the Navy Chevrolet of Greg Sacks, the Marines Pontiac of Buddy Baker, the Air Force Pontiac of Mickey Gibbs, and the Coast Guard Chevrolet of Dave Marcis. Kulwicki led the troops with an eighth-place finish. **3.** Bill Elliott, running his family's #9 Coors Light Ford for the final year, leads the Junior Johnson-owned Fords of Geoffrey Bodine (#11) and Sterling Marlin (#22) during the Daytona 500. Elliott would team with Johnson in 1992. While both Elliott and Bodine finished back in the pack, Marlin posted a second-place finish. **4.** Dale Earnhardt (#3) leads the Roush Racing #6 Ford of Mark Martin during the Daytona 500. Martin, running in his seventh 500, matched his best finish at the time, 21st. **5.** Running on the apron to conserve fuel, Ernie Irvan takes the checkered

3.

4.

5.

6.

7.

flag in the Morgan-McClure #4 Kodak Chevrolet to win the 1991 Daytona 500. Dale Earnhardt crashed with two laps remaining—shortly after losing the lead to Irvan—causing the race to end under caution. Finishing a close second was Sterling Marlin in Junior Johnson's #22 Maxwell House Ford. Marlin would join with Morgan-McClure two years later to give the team two additional Daytona 500 victories. **6.** Ernie Irvan enjoyed a "picture perfect" run in the Morgan-McClure #4 Kodak Chevrolet. **7.** Ernie Irvan opened his second full-time season in NASCAR's top series by winning the biggest event of the year, the Daytona 500. Irvan's second career victory quickly elevated him to the ranks of NASCAR front-runners.

> **"I was looking at the scoreboard when the engine sputtered. I said, 'Oh no, this can't be happening!' I dropped down on the banking and it didn't pick up again until Turn 3. I think I won the one I needed to win."**
>
> —Ernie Irvan

Ernie Irvan #4 Chevrolet

2. Sterling Marlin — Ford
3. Joe Ruttman — Oldsmobile
4. Rick Mast — Oldsmobile
5. Dale Earnhardt — Chevrolet
6. Dale Jarrett — Ford
7. Bobby Hillin Jr. — Oldsmobile
8. Alan Kulwicki — Ford
9. Ricky Rudd — Chevrolet
10. Bobby Hamilton — Oldsmobile

125-Mile Qualifying Race winners:
Davey Allison, Dale Earnhardt

1.

2.

1. Dale Earnhardt (center) poses with a group of sponsor VIPs after scoring his third consecutive victory in the Gatorade Twin 125-Mile Qualifying Races. His hopes of finally winning the Daytona 500 were dashed when he hit an errant ring-billed gull in the opening laps, disturbing the handling of his Chevrolet. That was one of only four times in 23 starts that he failed to lead the Daytona 500. 2. In 1992, NASCAR fans bid farewell to "The King" with a series of celebrations honoring Richard Petty in his final season of competition. He finished 16th in his 32nd and final Daytona 500. 3. Alan Kulwicki races Derrike Cope during the Daytona 500. Kulwicki, the owner/driver of the #7 Hooters Ford Thunderbird, needed a provisional start to make the field for the Daytona 500 but went on to finish fourth. Kulwicki won two races and edged Bill Elliott by 10 points to win the 1992 NASCAR championship. Cope, returning in Bob Whitcomb's #10 Purolator Chevrolet, suffered a cracked radiator and finished 34th. 4. Four years after finishing second behind his father, Davey Allison drove the Robert Yates Racing #28 Texaco Havoline Ford to victory in the Daytona 500. Bobby and Davey Allison became the second father-son combination to win the event, joining Lee and Richard Petty. 5. Davey Allison (#28) takes the checkered flag to win the 1992 Daytona 500, holding off the Wood Brothers #21 Citgo Ford of Morgan Shepherd.

3.

"All hell broke loose behind me. A year ago I probably would have been right in the middle of it. Maybe I've grown up a little bit. As far as wins go, this is the best one I've ever had."

—Davey Allison

4.

5.

Davey Allison #28 Ford

2. Morgan Shepherd   Ford
3. Geoffrey Bodine   Ford
4. Alan Kulwicki   Ford
5. Dick Trickle   Oldsmobile
6. Kyle Petty   Pontiac
7. Terry Labonte   Oldsmobile
8. Ted Musgrave   Chevrolet
9. Dale Earnhardt   Chevrolet
10. Phil Parsons   Ford

125-Mile Qualifying Race winners:
Dale Earnhardt, Bill Elliott

1993

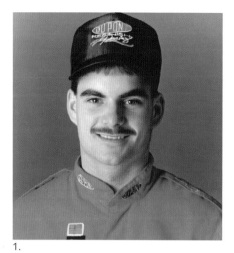

1.

2.

3.

1. Jeff Gordon made his first start in NASCAR's top series in the 1992 season finale at Atlanta—which was also Richard Petty's final race. During the 1993 Speedweeks, Gordon won the opening Gatorade Twin 125-Mile Qualifying Race and led the opening lap of the Daytona 500 driving Rick Hendrick's #24 DuPont Chevrolet. He went on to finish fifth. **2.** Polesitter Kyle Petty leads the field at the start of the 1993 Daytona 500 By STP in Felix Sabates' #42 Mello Yello Pontiac. He is joined by Dale Jarrett, driving the Joe Gibbs #18 Interstate Batteries Chevrolet, with the Chevrolets of Jeff Gordon (#24) and Dale Earnhardt (#3) in the second row. **3.** Rusty Wallace goes for a wild ride down the backstretch in Roger Penske's #2 Miller Genuine Draft Pontiac. Phil Parsons manages to get by in Larry Hedrick's #41 Manheim Auctions Chevrolet. Wallace also had a bad flip at the same location during a qualifying race in 1983.

4.

5.

> "This is hard to believe! I'm one of the most fortunate individuals in the world—to win three Super Bowls and now, the Super Bowl of motorsports."
> —Joe Gibbs

4. Dale Earnhardt (#3) led the Daytona 500 at the white flag for the second time in four years, and again victory evaded him. This time, #18 Dale Jarrett—with drafting help from #15 Geoffrey Bodine—took the lead exiting Turn 2 and went on to beat Earnhardt to the checkered flag. **5.** With his dad (two-time NASCAR champion Ned Jarrett) cheering him on for a national television audience, Dale Jarrett (#18) beats Dale Earnhardt to the checkered flag by a car length to win the 1993 Daytona 500. Third, in the Bud Moore #15 Motorcraft Ford, is Geoffrey Bodine, while Hut Stricklin, in Junior Johnson's #27 McDonald's Ford, edges rookie Jeff Gordon (#24) for fourth. The race for sixth is also close, with Mark Martin (#6) taking the position from Morgan Shepherd (#21). **6.** Joe Gibbs (right), who coached the Washington Redskins to three NFL Super Bowl victories, won the biggest stock car race of the year with Dale Jarrett. It was the first NASCAR victory for Gibbs, who began fielding a team in NASCAR's top series in 1992—the year he won his third Super Bowl.

6.

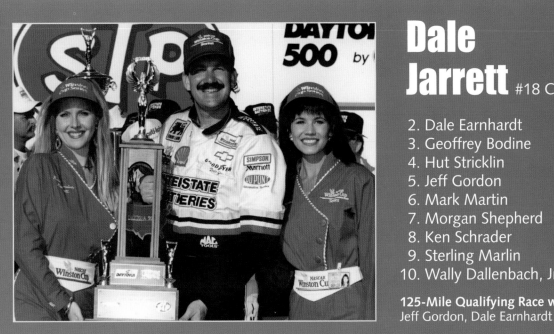

Dale Jarrett #18 Chevrolet

2.	Dale Earnhardt	Chevrolet
3.	Geoffrey Bodine	Ford
4.	Hut Stricklin	Ford
5.	Jeff Gordon	Chevrolet
6.	Mark Martin	Ford
7.	Morgan Shepherd	Ford
8.	Ken Schrader	Chevrolet
9.	Sterling Marlin	Ford
10.	Wally Dallenbach, Jr.	Ford

125-Mile Qualifying Race winners:
Jeff Gordon, Dale Earnhardt

1994

1.

1. Qualifying resulted in a surprise winner of the pole for the 36th Annual Daytona 500. Loy Allen Jr. in the #19 Ford ran a lap of 190.158 mph to become the first rookie to capture the pole for NASCAR's premier event. Allen never led during the race and finished 22nd, two laps down. **2.** Ken Schrader, driving Rick Hendrick's #25 Chevrolet, drew the pole for the 1994 Busch Clash, featuring pole winners from the 1993 season. P.J. Jones started second, followed by Dale Earnhardt, Geoffrey Bodine, and Mark Martin. While Earnhardt won the first segment, sixth-place starter Jeff Gordon won the non-points paying event. **3.** Car owner Felix Sabates (right) talks with Joe Nemechek. Beginning his rookie season, Nemechek finished 16th in his qualifying race to miss his first Daytona 500 by one position. While Sabates owned Kyle Petty's Pontiac in 1994, he signed Nemechek to drive when Petty rejoined his family operation three years later. **4.** Sterling Marlin (right) is ready to lend a hand while two Morgan-McClure Motorsports crewmen work on the #4 Kodak Chevrolet Lumina. Marlin joined the team at the beginning of the year, moving over from the #8 Ford fielded by the Stavola Brothers. Marlin's place on that team was taken by rookie Jeff Burton.

2.

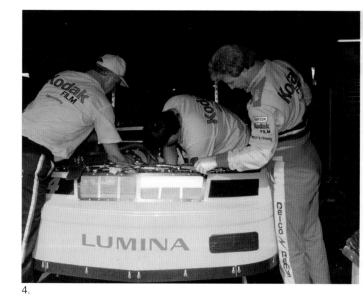

3.

4.

5.

5. In a reversal of the 1991 Daytona 500 finish, Sterling Marlin beats Ernie Irvan to the checkered flag. Irvan was at the wheel of the Morgan-McClure #4 Kodak Chevrolet in the team's initial Daytona 500 victory, but left to join Robert Yates Racing's #28 Texaco Havoline Ford to replace the late Davey Allison, who died in a helicopter accident the previous July. 6. Crewmen from rival teams line up to congratulate Sterling Marlin on his Daytona 500 victory. Marlin began racing at NASCAR's top level in 1976, when he substituted for his father, Coo Coo Marlin. It was his first NASCAR victory, which came in his first start for Morgan-McClure Motorsports.

6.

Sterling Marlin #4 Chevrolet

2. Ernie Irvan	Ford
3. Terry Labonte	Chevrolet
4. Jeff Gordon	Chevrolet
5. Morgan Shepherd	Ford
6. Greg Sacks	Ford
7. Dale Earnhardt	Chevrolet
8. Ricky Rudd	Ford
9. Bill Elliott	Ford
10. Ken Schrader	Chevrolet

125-Mile Qualifying Race winners:
Ernie Irvan, Dale Earnhardt

1995

1.

2.

3.

1. Sterling Marlin beats Darrell Waltrip to the checkered flag to win the first Gatorade Twin 125-Mile Qualifying Race. Three days later, Marlin became the sixth driver to follow up a qualifying race victory by winning the Daytona 500. **2.** Dale Earnhardt won his eighth career and sixth consecutive Gatorade Twin 125-Mile Qualifying Race. He is shown with Racestopper Lisa Shrowder (left), wife Teresa (right) and daughter Taylor Nicole, **3.** The RahMoc Racing pit crew services the Ford of Todd Bodine. Making his first Daytona 500 start, Bodine joined older brothers Geoffrey and Brett in the field. While the youngest Bodine started 11th and

4.

5

led seven laps, he went out before the 200-mile mark and finished 36th. **4.** Sterling Marlin, driving the #4 Kodak Chevrolet, leads Bobby Labonte, Jeff Gordon, Robert Pressley, and Dale Earnhardt during the Daytona 500. The five are racing Monte Carlos, which replaced the Lumina nameplate in 1995. **5.** Sterling Marlin in the #4 Kodak Chevrolet is winning the race off pit road, being chased by Dale Earnhardt's #3 Goodwrench Chevrolet and Ken Schrader in the #25 Budweiser Chevrolet. Marlin led the final 20 laps of the Daytona 500, beating Earnhardt to the checkered flag by .61 second. **6.** CBS announcer Mike Joy (in blue shirt at left) is standing by as Sterling Marlin smiles for the cameras after stepping out of his car in Victory Lane following his second consecutive victory in the Daytona 500.

6.

Sterling Marlin #4 Chevrolet

2.	Dale Earnhardt	Chevrolet
3.	Mark Martin	Ford
4.	Ted Musgrave	Ford
5.	Dale Jarrett	Ford
6.	Michael Waltrip	Pontiac
7.	Steve Grissom	Chevrolet
8.	Terry Labonte	Chevrolet
9.	Ken Schrader	Chevrolet
10.	Morgan Shepherd	Ford

125-Mile Qualifying Race winners:
Sterling Marlin, Dale Earnhardt

1996

1.

2.

1. Dale Earnhardt won his only Busch Pole Award for the Daytona 500 in 1996, running a lap of 189.510 mph in the Richard Childress #3 GM Goodwrench Chevrolet. He followed that up with his seventh consecutive victory in the Gatorade Twin 125-Mile Qualifying Races. **2.** Ernie Irvan, on the comeback trail, noses out the Hendrick Motorsports #25 Bud Chevrolet of Ken Schrader to win the second Gatorade Twin 125-Mile Qualifying Race. Irvan was injured in a practice crash at Michigan in August 1994 but scored two top-10 finishes in three races late in 1995. For 1996, Irvan returned to the #28 Texaco Havoline Ford, with teammate Dale Jarrett switching to the #88 Quality Care Ford. **3.** Bidding to become the first driver to score three consecutive victories in the Daytona 500, Sterling Marlin leads the field in the Morgan-McClure #4 Kodak Chevrolet, chased by Jeff Gordon, Dale Jarrett, and Dale Earnhardt. Marlin led laps 77–79, but his engine blew only two laps later, resulting in a 40th-place finish. **4.** John Andretti's #37 Little Caesars Ford bounces off the wall in a crash on lap 130.

3.

4.

5.

5. With Ernie Irvan's return to the Robert Yates Racing #28 Texaco Havoline Ford, Dale Jarrett lost his ride. Ford stepped up to sponsor the #88 Thunderbird for Jarrett in 1996. 6. Jarrett shows his appreciation to Ford and his team by scoring his second career victory in "The Great American Race." Chasing him to the checkered flag are Dale Earnhardt—a Daytona 500 bridesmaid for the third time in four years—Ken Schrader, Mark Martin, and Jeff Burton.

6.

Dale
Jarrett #88 Ford

2.	Dale Earnhardt	Chevrolet
3.	Ken Schrader	Chevrolet
4.	Mark Martin	Ford
5.	Jeff Burton	Ford
6.	Wally Dallenbach Jr.	Ford
7.	Ted Musgrave	Ford
8.	Bill Elliott	Ford
9.	Ricky Rudd	Ford
10.	Michael Waltrip	Ford

125-Mile Qualifying Race winners:
Dale Earnhardt, Ernie Irvan

1997

1.

2.

1. Continuing an incredible streak, Dale Earnhardt (#3) takes his eighth consecutive—and 10th career—victory in the Gatorade Twin 125-Mile Qualifying Races. Chasing him to the line are Jeff Gordon (#24), Bill Elliott (#94), and Ken Schrader (#33). **2.** Once again, Dale Earnhardt (#3) appeared to be the man to beat in the Daytona 500. He took the lead from pole-sitting teammate Mike Skinner on the second lap and led the next 49 circuits. Drivers chasing Earnhardt in early action include Skinner (#31), Bill Elliott (#94), Ken Schrader (#33), Sterling Marlin (#4), Jeff Gordon

(#24), Dale Jarrett (#88), Mark Martin (#6), Steve Grissom (#41), Michael Waltrip (#21), and Rusty Wallace (#2). **3.** With the laps winding down, Dale Earnhardt (#3) leads a group of drivers including Dale Jarrett (#88), Rusty Wallace (#2), Michael Waltrip (#21), and Mike Skinner (#31). **4.** Dale Earnhardt's chances of winning the Daytona 500 were suddenly dashed on lap 189. Moments after being passed by Jeff Gordon for second place behind leader Bill Elliott, Earnhardt (#3) glanced off the wall and began a wild, upside-down ride. Terry Labonte (#5, right) managed to get by without damage

3.

4.

5. After his car landed on its wheels following his lap 189 incident, Dale Earnhardt walked to the ambulance. Noticing that the wheels were still on the car, Earnhardt asked a safety worker to see if the engine would start. When it fired up, Earnhardt got back into the damaged car, drove to the pits, and managed to finish the race, although five laps down in 31st position.

5.

1997

1.

1. Crew chief Ray Evernham (left) and Jeff Gordon get a look at the competition from atop the Hendrick Motorsports hauler. 2. The Hendrick Motorsports teammates take the checkered flag in a three-abreast finish. Lake Speed and John Andretti spun on the backstretch to cause the final lap to be run under caution. Jeff Gordon won in the #24 DuPont Chevrolet, flanked by the #5 Kellogg's Chevrolet of Terry Labonte and the #25 Budweiser Chevrolet of Ricky Craven. Bill Elliott took fourth in his own #94 McDonald's Ford, followed by Sterling Marlin in the #4 Kodak Chevrolet. 3. Jeff Gordon pumps his fist for the crowd after winning his first Daytona 500. 4. Runner-up Terry Labonte (left) and third-place finisher Ricky Craven flank Daytona 500 winner Jeff Gordon in Victory Lane. It was an emotional finish for the Hendrick Motorsports teammates, whose car owner, Rick Hendrick, had recently been diagnosed with leukemia. 5. Jeff Gordon holds the Harley Earl Award while posing in front of the Harley J. Earl Trophy in Victory Lane. This was the final time that the three-foot award would be presented. Future Daytona 500 winners would get a miniature replica of the permanent trophy.

2.

3.

4.

5.

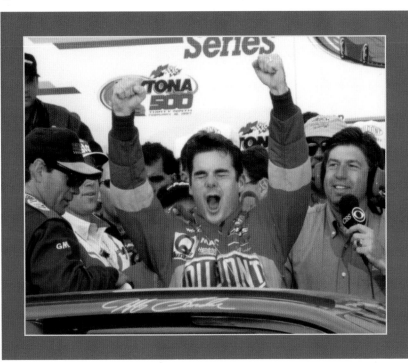

Jeff
Gordon #24 Chevrolet

2. Terry Labonte   Chevrolet
3. Ricky Craven   Chevrolet
4. Bill Elliott   Ford
5. Sterling Marlin   Chevrolet
6. Jeremy Mayfield   Ford
7. Mark Martin   Ford
8. Ward Burton   Pontiac
9. Ricky Rudd   Ford
10. Darrell Waltrip   Chevrolet

125-Mile Qualifying Race winners:
Dale Jarrett, Dale Earnhardt

1998

1.

2.

1. It seemed the only thing Dale Earnhardt was missing in the Daytona 500 was luck. When a nine-year-old girl from the Make-A-Wish Foundation gave him a lucky penny the morning of the race, Earnhardt glued it to the dash of his Chevrolet. **2.** Early action sees Bobby Labonte, driving the pole-winning Joe Gibbs Racing Pontiac, leading Sterling Marlin in the #40 Chevrolet, Dale Earnhardt in the #3 Chevrolet, Dale Jarrett in the #88 Ford, and Derrike Cope in the #36 Pontiac. **3.** Cars stack up two- and three-wide behind Dale Earnhardt and Ernie Irvan in action during the Daytona 500. **4.** Dale Jarrett started fifth in the Robert Yates Racing #88 Quality Care Ford but was never a factor in a bid for his third Daytona 500 triumph. He fin-

ished 34th, four laps down. **5.** Dale Earnhardt leads Ernie Irvan, Jeremy Mayfield, Rusty Wallace, and Jeff Gordon in the Daytona 500. Penske Racing South had a good race, with the #12 Mobil 1 and #2 Miller Lite Fords of Mayfield and Wallace running with the leaders all day and finishing in the top five. **6.** Dale Earnhardt has help from teammate Mike Skinner to draft past Jeff Gordon's #24 DuPont Chevrolet to take the lead on lap 123. Gordon led twice in a bid to repeat as Daytona 500 champion but got shuffled back to finish 16th. **7.** Dale Earnhardt was the class of the Daytona 500 field in Richard Childress' #3 GM Goodwrench Plus Chevrolet Monte Carlo. He led for 107 laps, including the final 61.

3.

4.

6.

5.

7.

1998

1.

2.

1. Dale Earnhardt managed to dodge many obstacles—including broken pieces of bellhousing and low-flying gulls—on his way to taking the checkered flag to win the Daytona 500. 2. In recognition of Dale Earnhardt's years of trying to win NASCAR's greatest race, members of the pit crews participating in the event lined pit road to offer congratulations following the race. 3. Dale Earnhardt delighted the fans by burning a doughnut in the shape of his #3 in the tri-oval grass. 4. A triumphant Dale Earnhardt stands atop his winning Chevrolet in Victory Lane. Usually a man in a hurry, Earnhardt's years of frustration led to a lengthy celebration. 5. NASCAR President Bill France, Jr., offers his congratulations to Dale Earnhardt in the International Speedway Corporation Suite. The celebration continued several hours after the waving of the checkered flag.

3.

5.

4.

A DETERMINED EARNHARDT FINALLY BREAKS THROUGH

No one has ever run Daytona International Speedway like Dale Earnhardt. He is the Speedway's all-time leading winner with 34 victories—more than twice as many as runner-up Bobby Allison. Over the years, Earnhardt had racked up a couple of victories in the Firecracker 400, six each in both the Budweiser Shootout and International Race of Champions, and a dozen Gatorade 125-mile qualifying races. The only race he just couldn't seem to win was the big one: the Daytona 500.

So many times he came so close. Yet year after year, something different would snatch away the victory. But he kept coming back, ever more determined to one day have his name engraved on the Harley J. Earl Trophy.

In his first Daytona 500 in 1979, Earnhardt led five times en route to a promising eighth-place finish. The following year, he won the Busch Clash and seemed to have an open invitation in the 500 to visit Gatorade Victory Lane. His invitation, however, expired late in the race.

In 1986, Earnhardt led the Daytona 500 on six occasions, only to have his engine quit three laps from the finish. The following year, he was leading with 11 laps remaining when he had to pit for fuel. "To get that close and miss would have really wrecked a lot of teams and ruined an entire season, but it just made the guys on our crew work harder," Earnhardt admitted after the latter loss. Hard enough, apparently, to help Earnhardt to his third championship.

While Earnhardt consistently dominated Speedweeks events, he continued to experience misfortune in the Daytona 500. In 1990, Earnhardt was only two turns from winning "The Great American Race" when he ran over a stray piece of bellhousing and cut a tire. Forced to slow entering Turn 3, he was passed by a surprised and delighted Derrike Cope. The next year, he and Davey Allison crashed two laps from the finish. In '93 he was passed by Dale Jarrett for the lead on the final lap.

Sometimes, he just experienced bad luck. His 1992 hopes were dashed when he hit an errant ring-billed gull in the opening laps, disturbing the handling of his Chevrolet. That was one of only four times in 23 starts that Earnhardt failed to lead a lap in the Daytona 500, although he went on to finish ninth.

Other near misses haunted him in 1995 and '96, when Earnhardt finished a close second behind Sterling Marlin and Dale Jarrett, respectively. In 1997, Earnhardt was running second with 11 laps remaining when he touched the wall coming off Turn 2, was hit from behind, and began a series of rolls in front of the Superstretch grandstands.

"It's time for the luck to go our way," Earnhardt said prior to the 1998 Daytona 500. "Seems like everybody else has been in those positions and had that luck run their way."

And finally, it did. Nothing arose during the 1998 Daytona 500 that could deny him, as he led 107 of the 200 laps—including the final 61—and the checkered flag flew to welcome Earnhardt's black #3 Chevrolet to Gatorade Victory Lane. In a fitting celebration, he carved a pair of doughnuts in the tri-oval grass to form the number "3." Afterward, other race teams lined pit road to high-five the man known as "The Intimidator" in a group congratulation for a victory well earned—and long in coming.

Dale Earnhardt #3 Chevrolet

2. Bobby Labonte	Pontiac
3. Jeremy Mayfield	Ford
4. Ken Schrader	Chevrolet
5. Rusty Wallace	Ford
6. Ernie Irvan	Pontiac
7. Chad Little	Ford
8. Mike Skinner	Chevrolet
9. Michael Waltrip	Ford
10. Bill Elliott	Ford

125-Mile Qualifying Race winners:
Sterling Marlin, Dale Earnhardt

.1.

2.

3.

1. Mark Martin is one of the greatest drivers never to win the Daytona 500. Martin's lone victory in NASCAR's top series at Daytona was in the 1999 Bud Shootout. He managed to win the NASCAR Craftsman Truck Series race in 2006, won a pair of IROC events, and triumphed in his class four times in the Rolex 24 at Daytona sports car race.
2. Dale Earnhardt, driving the #3 GM Goodwrench Chevrolet, leads a six-car draft during the second Gatorade Twin 125-mile qualifying race. Dale Jarrett runs second in the #88 Ford, followed by Penske Racing Ford teammates Jeremy Mayfield and Rusty Wallace, rookie Tony Stewart in the Joe Gibbs Racing #20 Home Depot Pontiac, and the #31 Chevrolet of Mike Skinner. **3.** Continuing an incredible streak, Dale Earnhardt celebrates his 10th consecutive victory in the Gatorade Twin 125s. It was also his 12th victory in the qualifying races for the Daytona 500 and his final NASCAR victory at the track. Earnhardt came back in 2000 to win the International Race of Champions season opener, giving him 34 career triumphs at Daytona International Speedway. Bobby Allison is second on the all-time list with 16 victories.
4. Dale Jarrett's #88 Ford spins to the inside after bumping Robert Yates Racing teammate Kenny Irwin Jr. (#28) on lap 135 of the Daytona 500, triggering an accident that involved more than a dozen cars. Irwin went on to finish a career-best third.

4.

5.

5. NASCAR's restrictor-plate and aerodynamic package produced plenty of three-abreast racing at the 1999 Daytona 500. Jeff Gordon, in the #24 Chevrolet, races to the inside of the #3 Chevrolet of Dale Earnhardt and the #99 Roush Racing Exide Ford of Jeff Burton. In the closing laps, the top 12 cars were separated by less than half a second. **6.** Jeff Gordon takes the checkered flag .128 second in front of Dale Earnhardt to score his second Daytona 500 victory. Third is the #28 Robert Yates Racing Texaco Havoline Ford of Kenny Irwin Jr., followed by the Lowe's Chevrolet of Mike Skinner.

6.

Jeff Gordon #24 Chevrolet

2.	Dale Earnhardt	Chevrolet
3.	Kenny Irwin Jr.	Ford
4.	Mike Skinner	Chevrolet
5.	Michael Waltrip	Chevrolet
6.	Ken Schrader	Chevrolet
7.	Kyle Petty	Pontiac
8.	Rusty Wallace	Ford
9.	Chad Little	Ford
10.	Rick Mast	Ford

125-Mile Qualifying Race winners:
Bobby Labonte, Dale Earnhardt

1.

1. Speedweeks was an uncharacteristic struggle for Dale Earnhardt (#3), whose car was dressed in a special orange paint scheme for the Daytona 500. While he won the IROC opener, he finished 11th in his qualifying race—ending a 10-year winning streak—and placed 21st in the Daytona 500, failing to lead a lap. Trying to help him along with a bump draft is his son, Dale Earnhardt Jr. (#8). **2.** In his rookie appearance at the Daytona 500, Dale Earnhardt Jr. (right) managed to finish fourth in his Gatorade Twin 125-Mile Qualifying Race, and then finished 13th in the Daytona 500—eight positions in front of his father. **3.** The Robert Yates Fords of Dale Jarrett (#88) and Ricky Rudd (#28) lead the field at the start of the Daytona 500, followed by the #94 Ford of Bill Elliott, the #31 Chevrolet of Mike Skinner, the #22 Pontiac of Ward Burton, the #2 Ford of Rusty Wallace, and the #8 Chevrolet of rookie Dale Earnhardt Jr. **4.** Running under yellow and being led by the silver Pontiac pace car, Dale Jarrett takes the checkered flag in the #88 Quality Care Ford to win his third Daytona 500. Second is Jeff Burton in Jack Roush's #99 Exide Ford, followed by Bill Elliott in his #94 McDonald's Ford. **5.** Car owner Robert Yates (center) celebrates his third Daytona 500 victory with driver Dale Jarrett (left) and crew chief Todd Parrott in Victory Lane.

2.

3.

4.

5.

Dale
Jarrett #88 Ford

2. Jeff Burton   Ford
3. Bill Elliott   Ford
4. Rusty Wallace   Ford
5. Mark Martin   Ford
6. Bobby Labonte   Pontiac
7. Terry Labonte   Chevrolet
8. Ward Burton   Pontiac
9. Ken Schrader   Pontiac
10. Matt Kenseth   Ford

125-Mile Qualifying Race winners:
Bill Elliott, Ricky Rudd

2001

1.

2.

3.

4.

1. Tony Stewart pays his first visit to Victory Lane at Daytona after winning the Budweiser Shootout for pole winners from the previous season. **2.** Jeff Gordon leads the pack past the expanded grandstands and tower at the start/finish line. Giving chase are Mark Martin, Sterling Marlin, Joe Nemechek, Jeff Burton, Bobby Labonte, pole winner Bill Elliott, Terry Labonte, Dale Jarrett, and Andy Houston. **3.** Dale Earnhardt's familiar #3 GM Goodwrench Chevrolet drafts the #96 McDonald's Ford of rookie Andy Houston. Driving a car owned by former CART Champ Car owner Cal Wells, Houston started ninth but retired after being involved in a lap 174 accident. **4.** Tony Stewart's Joe Gibbs Racing #20 Home Depot Pontiac is knocked into the air during a 19-car melee on lap 174. Stewart was shaken up but uninjured. The incident was triggered when the #4 Chevrolet of Robby Gordon tapped the #22 Dodge of Ward Burton. Dale Earnhardt manages to avoid the skirmish in his #3 Chevrolet. The Daytona 500 featured 49 lead changes among 14 drivers. **5.** Michael Waltrip, followed by DEI Chevrolet teammate Dale Earnhardt Jr. and car owner Dale Earnhardt, leads the field to the white flag. Among the cars giving chase are Sterling Marlin in the #40 Dodge, Ricky Rudd in the #28 Ford, Bobby Hamilton in the #55 Chevrolet, Rusty Wallace in the #2 Ford, Ken Schrader in the #36 Pontiac, and Mike Wallace in the #7 Ford. **6.** Michael Waltrip takes the checkered flag to win the 2001 Daytona 500, closely followed by DEI teammate Dale Earnhardt Jr. The yellow waved for NASCAR legend Dale Earnhardt, who tragically lost his life in a Turn 4 accident on the final lap. **7.** Not knowing the outcome of the last-lap incident that took place behind him, Michael Waltrip steps from the #15 NAPA Chevrolet to celebrate his Daytona 500 victory.

6.

"The only reason
I won this race is
Dale Earnhardt."

—Michael Waltrip

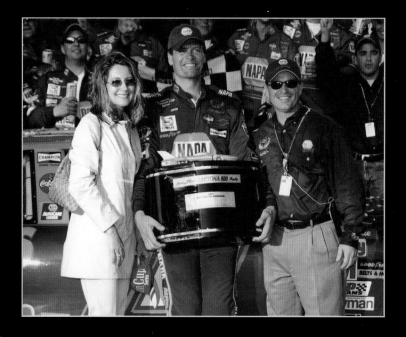

Michael Waltrip #15 Chevrolet

2. Dale Earnhardt Jr.   Chevrolet
3. Rusty Wallace   Ford
4. Ricky Rudd   Ford
5. Bill Elliott   Dodge
6. Mike Wallace   Ford
7. Sterling Marlin   Dodge
8. Bobby Hamilton   Chevrolet
9. Jeremy Mayfield   Ford
10. Stacy Compton   Dodge

125-Mile Qualifying Race winners:
Sterling Marlin, Mike Skinner

2002

1.

2.

3.

4.

1. With his #24 Chevrolet carrying a special DuPont 200 Years paint scheme, Jeff Gordon takes the checkered flag to win the first of the Gatorade 125s. Chasing him to the line are Dale Earnhardt Jr., Ken Schrader, and Ricky Rudd. **2.** Rookie pole winner Jimmie Johnson and Kevin Harvick lead the field for the start of the Daytona 500. Johnson won the pole with a lap of 185.831 mph in the #48 Lowe's Chevrolet owned by Rick Hendrick and Jeff Gordon. While Harvick replaced Dale Earnhardt at Richard Childress Racing, the team switched colors and numbers, going with the silver #29. **3.** Making his 33rd and final start in the Daytona 500, Dave Marcis finished 42nd in his #71 Realtree Chevrolet. He's racing the #12 Alltel Ford of rookie Ryan Newman, who drove to a seventh-place finish for car owner Roger Penske. **4.** Dale Earnhardt Jr., driving the #8 DEI Budweiser Chevrolet, races the #09 Miccosukee Chevrolet of Geoffrey Bodine. Unhappy with the team's progress early in the race, car owner James Finch had left for the Halifax Marina. He hurried back when Bodine fought his way into contention late in the race, finishing third. **5.** In a costly move, Sterling Marlin is about to touch the fender of his Chip Ganassi Racing #40 Coors Light Dodge as the field is stopped under the red flag with five laps remaining in the Daytona 500. Marlin pulled out the fender, which was rubbing against the tire due to being crumpled in a battle for the lead with Jeff Gordon, who spun to bring out the yellow and red flags. At this point, Marlin was in the lead but was black-flagged for working on his car during the race stoppage. Ward Burton, parked behind Marlin in second, then inherited the lead. Marlin fell to 14th but raced his way back to finish eighth.

5.

6. Ward Burton takes the checkered flag to win the Daytona 500 in the #22 Caterpillar Dodge fielded by Bill Davis Racing. Elliott Sadler finished second in the #21 Wood Brothers Ford, while Geoffrey Bodine finished a solid third in James Finch's #09 Miccosukee Ford. Bodine had worked himself in a position to win, but lost his chances when his aerodynamics were damaged in an incident with Jeff Gordon with five laps remaining.

6.

Ward Burton #22 Dodge

2.	Elliott Sadler	Ford
3.	Geoffrey Bodine	Ford
4.	Kurt Busch	Ford
5.	Michael Waltrip	Chevrolet
6.	Mark Martin	Ford
7.	Ryan Newman	Ford
8.	Sterling Marlin	Dodge
9.	Jeff Gordon	Chevrolet
10.	Johnny Benson	Pontiac

125-Mile Qualifying Race winners:
Jeff Gordon, Michael Waltrip

2003

1.

2.

3.

4.

1. Pre-race festivities included a giant "USA" card trick, involving both the main and Superstretch grandstands, that was conducted under ominous skies. 2. The Superstretch grandstands—overlooking Lake Lloyd—boosted the capacity of Daytona International Speedway to more than 200,000. 3. Jeff Gordon meets John Travolta and his wife, Kelly Preston, along with skateboarding legend Tony Hawk during driver introductions. 4. Part of the giant crowd watches Michael Waltrip lead the Daytona 500. 5. Racing in huge packs is exciting for the fans but nerve-racking for the drivers. This contact between Ken Schrader and Ryan Newman in Turn 4 led to a four-car accident on lap 57. 6. Ryan Newman escaped injury in an accident in the tri-oval grass on lap 57 in the Penske South #12 Alltel Dodge. 7. Jeff Green won the pole with a lap of 186.606 mph in the #30 AOL Chevrolet. However, his day ended on lap 95 when he crashed with Jimmy Spencer in Turn 4. 8. Michael Waltrip, in the DEI #15 NAPA Chevrolet, races the Andy Petree Racing #33 Monaco Chevrolet of open-wheel veteran Christian Fittipaldi, followed by Kurt Busch in the Roush Racing #97 Rubbermaid Ford. Waltrip and Busch eventually finished 1-2. 9. Only four laps after Michael Waltrip took the lead from Jimmie Johnson, the Daytona 500 was red-flagged on lap 109 because of rain. Waltrip and his wife, Buffy, were kept in suspense for nearly two hours before the race was declared official.

5.

5.

7.

3.

9.

Michael
Waltrip #15 Chevrolet

2. Kurt Busch   Ford
3. Jimmie Johnson   Chevrolet
4. Kevin Harvick   Chevrolet
5. Mark Martin   Ford
6. Robby Gordon   Chevrolet
7. Tony Stewart   Chevrolet
8. Jeremy Mayfield   Dodge
9. Mike Wallace   Dodge
10. Dale Jarrett   Ford

125-Mile Qualifying Race winners:
Robby Gordon, Dale Earnhardt Jr.

2004

1.

2.

1. Dale Jarrett won the Bud Shootout for 2003 pole winners in the Robert Yates Racing #88 UPS Ford, held under the lights Saturday evening to open Speedweeks. Dale Earnhardt Jr. finished second, followed by Kevin Harvick and Mark Martin. **2.** The 2004 Daytona 500 ushered in a new era as NEXTEL became the sponsor of NASCAR's top series. The Daytona 500 featured a star-studded NEXTEL Tribute to America during the opening ceremonies. **3.** Dale Earnhardt Jr. and Elliott Sadler lead the field at the start of the Daytona 500. Greg Biffle won the pole with a lap of 188.387 mph in the #16 Roush Racing Ford but had to start from the back after changing engines.
4. The pack of cars led by Tony Stewart, Matt Kenseth, and Ricky Craven are dwarfed by *Air Force One*, parked at near-by Daytona Beach International Airport.
5. Multi-car packs featuring two- and three-wide racing have become the norm in the Daytona 500. Elliott Sadler, driving a gray #38 M&M's Ford for Robert Yates Racing, leads the #33 Chevrolet of Mike Skinner, the #30 Chevrolet of Johnny Sauter, and the rest of the pack. Dale Earnhardt Jr.'s Chevrolet is leading the middle line, pushed along by pole winner Greg Biffle in the #16 National Guard Ford, who came from the back of the pack at the start of the race. **6.** Jamie McMurray in the #42 Havoline Dodge and Michael Waltrip in the #15 NAPA Chevrolet lead the way, with Jeff Burton's #99 Ford, Jeff Gordon's #24 Chevrolet, and Bobby Labonte's #18 Chevrolet in hot pursuit. Burton's Ford carries a special paint scheme to promote TNT's coverage of the NBA All-Star Game later that evening.

3.

4.

5.

6.

2004

"He [Dale Earnhardt] was over in the passenger side with me. I'm sure he was having a blast. Some of our greatest competitors come in and out of this sport without taking this trophy home. I'm glad I can say I've accomplished it. We really wanted to win it so bad. Winning a race during Speedweeks makes you quite a bit more valuable in the sport as a driver."

—Dale Earnhardt Jr.

1.

1. Restrictor-plate racing not only featured giant packs on the speedway, it resulted in massive congestion on pit road, especially during caution periods. Rookie Brian Vickers is first in line to get service on the Hendrick Motorsports #25 ditech.com Chevrolet. **2.** Dale Earnhardt Jr.'s special paint scheme promoted Budweiser's "Born On Date" campaign. Earnhardt backed up his second consecutive 125-mile qualifying race victory by winning the Daytona 500. **3.** Dale Earnhardt Jr. takes the checkered flag .273 second ahead of Tony Stewart. Earnhardt led the final 20 circuits following a lap-181 restart after a 12-car crash. **4.** Enjoying one of the perks provided by the new series sponsor, Dale Earnhardt Jr. holds up a custom NEXTEL phone in Victory Lane. **5.** Runner-up Tony Stewart offers his congratulations to winner Dale Earnhardt Jr.

2.

4.

5.

3.

Dale Earnhardt Jr.

#8 Chevrolet

2. Tony Stewart   Chevrolet
3. Scott Wimmer   Dodge
4. Kevin Harvick   Chevrolet
5. Jimmie Johnson   Chevrolet
6. Joe Nemechek   Chevrolet
7. Elliott Sadler   Ford
8. Jeff Gordon   Chevrolet
9. Matt Kenseth   Ford
10. Dale Jarrett   Ford

125-Mile Qualifying Race winners:
Dale Earnhardt Jr., Elliott Sadler

2005

1.

2.

3.

4.

5.

1. Tony Stewart celebrates in Gatorade Victory Lane after winning the Gatorade Duel At Daytona. For 2005, the length of the qualifying races increased to 150 miles to ensure that pit stops would be needed. Michael Waltrip won the other Duel. **2.** An aerial view shows the sellout crowd at Daytona International Speedway. **3.** Dale Jarrett takes the green flag in the Robert Yates #88 UPS Ford after winning his third pole position for the Daytona 500. He gets drafting help from the #15 Chevrolet of Michael Waltrip, while second-fastest qualifier Jimmie Johnson's Chevrolet (#48) gets a push from the #20 Chevrolet of Tony Stewart. **4.** Part of the massive crowd watches Tony Stewart (#20) lead Michael Waltrip (#15) through the tri-oval past the start/finish line. Stewart had one of the cars to beat throughout much of the event, leading the race seven times. **5.** Jimmie Johnson (#48) and Dale Jarrett (#88) lead a 27-car pack through Turn 4. In the background is part of the Fan Walk, featuring manufacturers' displays and souvenir vendors. **6.** Jeff Gordon (#24) and Greg Biffle (#16) are at the front of a long line of cars in for service during a caution flag. Note the odd angle at which Dale Earnhardt Jr. had to squeeze into his pit farther down pit road. **7.** For the first time, the Daytona 500 finished at dusk—and also was extended into overtime. With debris spotted on the frontstretch on lap 199, the race went to a green/white/checker finish. Gordon held off Kurt Busch by .158 second, with Dale Earnhardt Jr. in third. Gordon passed Earnhardt for the lead on lap 198. "I didn't give up, but I thought it was over," Gordon said when Dale Jr. took the lead on lap 197. Dale Jr. countered: "Gordon was going by so fast I couldn't draft off the side of him ... he was gone." **8.** After winning the Daytona 500 for the second time, Jeff Gordon savored his 2005 triumph in Gatorade Victory Lane.

6.

7.

8.

Jeff Gordon #24 Chevrolet

2. Kurt Busch   Ford
3. Dale Earnhardt Jr.   Chevrolet
4. Scott Riggs   Chevrolet
5. Jimmie Johnson   Chevrolet
6. Mark Martin   Ford
7. Tony Stewart   Chevrolet
8. Sterling Marlin   Dodge
9. Kevin Lepage   Dodge
10. Rusty Wallace   Dodge

150-Mile Qualifying Race winners:
Michael Waltrip, Tony Stewart

2006

1.

2.

1. Jeff Burton won the pole for the Daytona 500 with a lap of 189.151 mph in the Richard Childress Racing #31 Cingular Chevrolet. **2.** One of the biggest surprises of Speedweeks was recorded by rookie Denny Hamlin, the winner of the Budweiser Shootout at Daytona. The Virginian drove Joe Gibbs Racing's #11 FedEx Chevrolet to victory ahead of Chevrolet veterans Tony Stewart and Dale Earnhardt Jr. **3.** Pole-sitter Jeff Burton holds the early lead in the Daytona 500. **4.** Another sell-out crowd watches the start of the Daytona 500. **5.** Carl Edwards, driving Jack Roush's #99 Office Depot Ford, tangles with the Petty Enterprises #45 Dodge of Kyle Petty as part of a six-car incident on lap 79. Edwards finished last in the 43-car field, while Petty was able to continue and finished 39th. **6.** Daytona 500 action sees former open-wheel star Robby Gordon, in his #7 Jim Beam Ford, battle the Ray Evernham #9 Dodge of Kasey Kahne and the Hendrick Motorsports #25 GMAC Chevrolet of Brian Vickers. **7.** With the race starting later in the afternoon, cars cast shadows on the banking as the Daytona 500 extends into the evening. Jimmie Johnson leads this 23-car pack. The tight racing saw 31 cars complete all 203 laps, with 34 drivers going 500 miles. **8.** The Daytona 500 finished under a green/white/checker for the second consecutive year. Jimmie Johnson took the yellow and checkered flags at the conclusion of lap 203, followed by Casey Mears and Ryan Newman. NASCAR dropped its "gentlemen's agreement" allowing competitors to race back to the caution, even on the last lap, and the caution waved when Greg Biffle crashed in Turn 4 on the final lap.

3.

4.

5.

6.

7.

8.

Jimmie Johnson #48 Chevrolet

2. Casey Mears   Dodge
3. Ryan Newman   Dodge
4. Elliott Sadler   Ford
5. Tony Stewart   Chevrolet
6. Clint Bowyer   Chevrolet
7. Brian Vickers   Chevrolet
8. Dale Earnhardt Jr.   Chevrolet
9. Ken Schrader   Ford
10. Dale Jarrett   Ford

150-Mile Qualifying Race winners:
Elliott Sadler, Jeff Gordon

2007

1.

2.

3.

1. Robert Yates Racing swept the front row for the Daytona 500. David Gilliland (right) was the surprise pole winner after running a lap of 186.320 mph in the #38 M&M's Ford Fusion. Veteran Ricky Rudd qualified second in the team's #88 Snickers entry. **2.** Getting plenty of attention at Daytona was Juan Pablo Montoya, a Colombian who left Formula One racing—where he was a seven-time winner—to run a full NASCAR schedule. Montoya drove for Chip Ganassi, his car owner for the 1999 CART championship and 2000 Indianapolis 500 victory. **3.** The Daytona 500 marked the debut of Toyota at NASCAR's highest level. One of the new Camrys was driven by AJ Allmendinger, a five-time winner in 2006 Champ Car competition. He was one of 18 drivers failing to qualify. **4.** Tony Stewart celebrates his triumph in the opening Gatorade Duel at Daytona 150-mile qualifying race. The Chevrolet driver held off Dale Earnhardt Jr. to take the victory. **5.** Jeff Gordon wasn't smiling for long after winning the second 150-mile Gatorade Duel at Daytona qualifying race. His Chevrolet was found to be an inch too low in post-race inspection, putting him to the back of the field for the Daytona 500. **6.** New Toyota car owner/driver Michael Waltrip (center) got to smile with team drivers David Reutimann (left) and Dale Jarrett at the beginning of Speedweeks. The new team was embroiled in controversy throughout the week. A foreign substance was found in the intake manifold of Waltrip's Toyota, leading to confiscation of his car in addition to a $100,000 penalty and loss of 100 points. Waltrip went on to finish 30th in the Daytona 500, with Jarrett leading the Toyotas with a 22nd-place finish. Reutimann opened his rookie season by finishing 40th. **7.** Part of the crowd of nearly 200,000 watches the start for the Daytona 500.

4.

5.

6.

7.

1.

2.

1. The Ray Evernham Dodges of Kasey Kahne (#9) and Elliott Sadler (#19) battle the Ford of Greg Biffle (#16) and the pole-winning Ford of David Gilliland (#38). Sadler led the group with a sixth-place finish. 2. Intense three-wide racing under the lights in the late going of the Daytona 500 sees the Chevrolet of Dale Earnhardt Jr. racing to the inside of the Ford of Carl Edwards, while the #40 Dodge of David Stremme and the #16 Ford of Greg Biffle draft on the outside. Stremme, driving one of three Chip Ganassi Racing entries, finished 11th to lead the group. 3. Kevin Harvick (#29) noses ahead of Mark Martin as the Chevrolets race to the checkered flag at the conclusion of lap 202 of the Daytona 500. 4. For the third straight year, the Daytona 500 ended with a green/white/checker finish. With a multi-car accident beginning while Mark Martin and Kevin Harvick raced to the checkered flag, NASCAR held off a field-freezing caution flag. Martin was ahead at the time of the accident, but Harvick edged him out before crossing the finish line; the official margin of victory was .020 second, the closest Daytona 500 finish since Lee Petty's victory in the inaugural 1959 event. 5. Mark Martin had a new team for 2007, running a limited schedule for new NASCAR owner Bobby Ginn. He opened the year by nearly winning the Daytona 500. Taking the lead on lap 176, Martin paced the field all the way to the sprint to the checkered flag. 6. The Richard Childress Racing #29 Chevrolet of Kevin Harvick drives into Gatorade Victory Lane after winning the Daytona 500.

"That was a tremendous amount of fun. All I wanted was a chance to win the Daytona 500 and those guys gave me that chance, and you just can't ask for more than that. Coming off of Turn 4, there we were, right in the thick of things—in real contention to win the Daytona 500. For a racer, it just doesn't get much better than that. I really wanted to win that thing. They were going to have to pry it out of my fingers, man."

—Mark Martin

3.

4.

5.

6.

Kevin Harvick #29 Chevrolet

2.	Mark Martin	Chevrolet
3.	Jeff Burton	Chevrolet
4.	Mike Wallace	Chevrolet
5.	David Ragan	Ford
6.	Elliott Sadler	Dodge
7.	Kasey Kahne	Dodge
8.	David Gilliland	Ford
9.	Joe Nemechek	Chevrolet
10.	Jeff Gordon	Chevrolet

150-Mile Qualifying Race winners:
Tony Stewart, Kurt Busch

The Cars of Daytona

When NASCAR opened its Strictly Stock division in 1949, the cars racing in it were just that—strictly stock. And technical inspectors were on hand to make sure of it. In fact, the winner of the very first race was disqualified afterward for having stiffer-than-stock rear springs.

By the time the first Daytona 500 was run in 1959, the competing cars looked stock but carried some mechanical modifications—which is why some were able to safely lap the track at more than 140 mph, far faster than their street counterparts could. Bodies, frames, and basic engines had to be the same as for production cars, a dictum that helped fuel the horsepower race of the 1950s and '60s. Up into the mid-1970s, either the horsepower or displacement was typically emblazoned on the cars' hoods.

If you looked inside those 1959 competitors, you'd see a fairly stock interior; a photo in the 1961 section shows the inside of Lee Petty's Plymouth with its stock front seat. You'll also see it has a roll cage, something NASCAR mandated as a safety measure.

Starting in 1966, teams were allowed to modify their car's frame "for safety purposes." This opened the door for all kinds of modifications. Even the early cars running at Daytona typically sat lower than their street counterparts and had bigger tires, but now cars started to look even squattier. Eventually, the rules were changed to allow purpose-built, tubular racing chassis.

It was also about this time that some creative bodywork was being applied. Midway through the 1966 season, the Ford fielded by driver-turned-team-owner Junior Johnson was modified with a lowered roof, slanted-back windshield, sloped front fenders, and a high-riding tail—all in the interest of better aerodynamics. The following year, famed mechanic Smokey Yunick did Junior one better by entering a Chevrolet Chevelle—already a midsize car—that was rendered in roughly ⅞ scale. Both cars were allowed to run, but NASCAR quickly countered with body templates as part of the inspection process to ensure subsequent violations could be proven.

Horsepower had always been the dominant factor in racing, and during the 1960s, companies went to great lengths to make more of it. In 1964, Chrysler brought back the Hemi V8 from the 1950s in a larger, more powerful form. Its cars cleaned up on high-speed tracks like Daytona, where Richard Petty qualified at 20 mph faster than he had the year before. So dominant were these Dodges and Plymouths that Ford pulled out its factory-sponsored cars in protest, and what few Ford and General Motors independents still ran usually didn't have much of a chance. NASCAR then made the Hemi illegal for the 1965 season—on grounds it wasn't really a production engine—and then *Chrysler* pulled out of racing. That left a void Ford was only too happy to fill, and the company's cars won a record 32 straight NASCAR races in '65. The Hemis were allowed to return in '66, by which time the Fords were also packing more power, and things returned to normal.

As speeds increased, aerodynamics became ever more important. Ford sought to get an edge in 1969 with the

1.

2.

3.

1. A very stock-appearing Thunderbird (bottom), Oldsmobile (middle), and Chevrolet race in the 1959 Daytona 500. 2. Richard Petty's 1964 Plymouth hunkers down over its lowered suspension and fat tires. 3. Both the Ford Torino Talladega (top) and Dodge Daytona of 1970 sported tapered nosepieces for better aerodynamics. 4. Bill Elliott kneels next to his record-setting 1987 Thunderbird. 5. The restrictor plate has long been the speed governor of choice at NASCAR. 6. Regardless of nameplate, today's cars have very similar profiles. 7. The 50th running of the Daytona 500 will be the first using the Car of Tomorrow, shown during testing.

Torino Talladega and Mercury Cyclone, which had sloped nosepieces. Chrysler's inevitable counterstrike appeared as the Dodge Daytona and Plymouth Superbird, which went even further in the aerodynamics department with long, pointy noses and tall rear wings. NASCAR rules stated that a certain number of these special models had to be available to the public to make them "legal" for racing, and the obligatory low-production examples have since become prized collector's items.

In the case of all these cars, the aerodynamic ploys worked. Speeds at the faster tracks got so high that cars were becoming unstable and concerns over tire life arose, so steps were taken to slow them down. First, NASCAR mandated that the winged Chryslers be limited to engines of just 305 cubic inches (vs. 426–429 cubic inches), and that put an abrupt end to Chrysler's slippery shenanigans. Then NASCAR came up with a device to limit the rest. Enter the much-maligned restrictor plate.

Placed between the carburetor and intake manifold, restrictor plates reduced the amount of air-fuel mixture going to the cylinders, thus reducing power and top speed. At first, all cars were required to have them. Then, in 1971, the rules were changed so that engines up to 366-cid could run unrestricted, but anything larger had to use a plate. This spelled the beginning of the end for the big-block 426–429-cubic-inch engines previously used and, at the same time, the hood numbers that advertised them. By 1975, the limit was set at 358-cid for all engines, and the high-speed problem disappeared—for a while.

With the table leveled for all makes, General Motors returned to the hunt, and even American Motors took a brief and not entirely unsuccessful stab at NASCAR racing. In 1978, Oldsmobiles and Buicks were seen on the Daytona starting grid for the first time since the early '60s, and Pontiac returned in '81.

Since Detroit was "downsizing" its cars due to fuel-economy concerns, NASCAR adjusted its rules accordingly. For the 1981 Daytona 500, the wheelbase limit was lowered from 115 inches to 110, which corresponded to Detroit's new fleet of midsize coupes.

Despite the smaller cars and smaller engines, speeds once again crept up. In 1987, Bill Elliott qualified his Thunderbird for Daytona at a stunning 210.364 mph, following it up with a 212.809 mph run at Talladega. NASCAR responded to the frightening speeds at these two tracks by bringing back an old friend: the restrictor plate. Since then, nobody has reached 200 mph in qualifying at either track, and likely never will.

When General Motors switched all its midsize cars to front-wheel drive in the late 1980s, racing versions wore somewhat production-looking bodies atop traditional tubular rear-drive racing chassis. Similarly, when Ford dropped its rear-drive Thunderbird after 1997, it was replaced on the NASCAR circuit by a rear-drive chassis supporting a Taurus "coupe" body—the production version of which was a front-drive four-door sedan. To some, this marked a definitive end to what could in any way be considered "stock cars" in NASCAR racing.

Largely due to efforts aimed at keeping the sport competitive, current NASCAR racers have established specifications and nearly identically shaped bodies. That will be taken a step further when the new "Car of Tomorrow"—which was used at some tracks during 2007—makes its debut at NASCAR's premier venue for the 50th running of the Daytona 500 in 2008. It's hard to imagine a more fitting introduction to Daytona's next 50 years.

4.

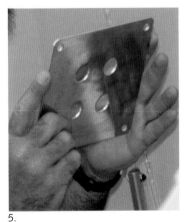

5.

6.

7.

Index